WOOL
the Australian Story

WOOL
the Australian Story

RICHARD WOLDENDORP

ROGER McDONALD

AMANDA BURDON

FREMANTLE ARTS CENTRE PRESS
IN ASSOCIATION WITH RICHARD WOLDENDORP

First published 2003 by
FREMANTLE ARTS CENTRE PRESS
in association with
RICHARD WOLDENDORP
PO Box 158, North Fremantle 6159
Western Australia.
www.facp.iinet.net.au

Designer John Douglass, Brown Cow Design.
Consultant Editor Janet Blagg.
Production Coordinator Vanessa Rycroft.

Typeset by Fremantle Arts Centre Press
and printed by Tein Wah Press, Singapore.

National Library of Australia
Cataloguing-in-publication data

Woldendorp, Richard, 1927–.
   Wool: the Australian story.

   ISBN 1 86368 396 8.

   1. Wool industry — Australia — History — Pictorial works.
   2. Wool industry — Australia — Pictorial works.
   I. McDonald, Roger, 1941– . II. Burdon, Amanda. III. Title.

338.17631450994

The State of Western Australia has made an investment in this project through
ArtsWA in association with the Lotteries Commission.

ACKNOWLEDGEMENTS

I first became familiar with the lives of Australian woolgrowers while compiling a book for the Royal Flying Doctor Service. I knew little of sheep or wool but could not help but admire the calibre of people who were willing to work under such extreme environmental conditions, and contend with such variations in product prices within the context of a precarious cost structure. It is but a glimpse of a rich and complex subject, but I hope this book will go some way to recognising the importance of the wool industry and its people to the Australian economy and our culture.

The book would not have been possible without the financial and logistical support of Wesfarmers Landmark. The company's involvement with the Australian wool industry traces back to the late 1840s when Frederick Dalgety began servicing producers in western Victoria. Today, Wesfarmers Landmark is one of Australia's largest wool brokers and marketers, servicing growers across the nation.

So many Landmark people provided so much help that it would be unfair to mention only some of those, from head office and branches across the country, who mustered me throughout my travels and to whom I am greatly indebted. But I would particularly like to mention Michael Chaney, CEO of Wesfarmers Limited, for his faith in the project.

In the field I was fortunate to have been welcomed into the lives and homes of many remarkable Australian wool producers and industry identities. I am especially grateful to Charles Massy, Larry Foley and Nan Broad for sharing their expertise and to the following people for their hospitality and technical advice: Judy and Tim Austin, Mark Baldwin, Doreen and Trevor Bignell, Chris Bowman, Graham Brown, Allen Cox, Ray Cubby, Andrew d'Espeissis, Noel Dawson, Angus and Donna Deane, Ron Denney, Ian Downie, James Ferguson, Brian and Mary Fraser, Marion Gibbons, Charles and Angela Good, Sally and George Hawker, Terry Heggaton, Bill Hughes, Penny and Kim Keogh, David Kininmonth, Carol-Ann Malouf, Jim Maple-Brown, the Maslen family, Mary McCrabb, Kim McDougall, Bob McFarland, Judith McGeorge, Clem McHaure, Hugh McLachlan, Jane and Locky McTaggart, Wally Merriman, Colleen and Malcolm Mitchell, Kerry Modystach, Kate and Cam Munro, Greg and Peter Munsie, Helen and Brett Pollock, Bob Reden, Denis and Marilyn Richmond, Peter Riley, Peter Ritter, Paul and Marlane Roe, John and Vera Taylor, Rod Thirkell-Johnston, Ross Tulley, Jill Vessey, Buddie Wagstaff, Judy White and Nancy Withers.

In terms of technical support I commend Malcolm McDonald of Custom Colour, Danny Comrie of QDI, John Douglass of Brown Cow Design, Ian Lloyd, as well as the Perth and Adelaide bases of the Royal Flying Doctor Service for their contributions to the book's production.

Finally, I applaud Amanda Burdon and Roger McDonald for their skilful wording and teamwork, and thank them for their support. A special thanks also to my wife, Lyn, and our daughter, Eva, for their day-to-day assistance and encouragement.

Richard Woldendorp

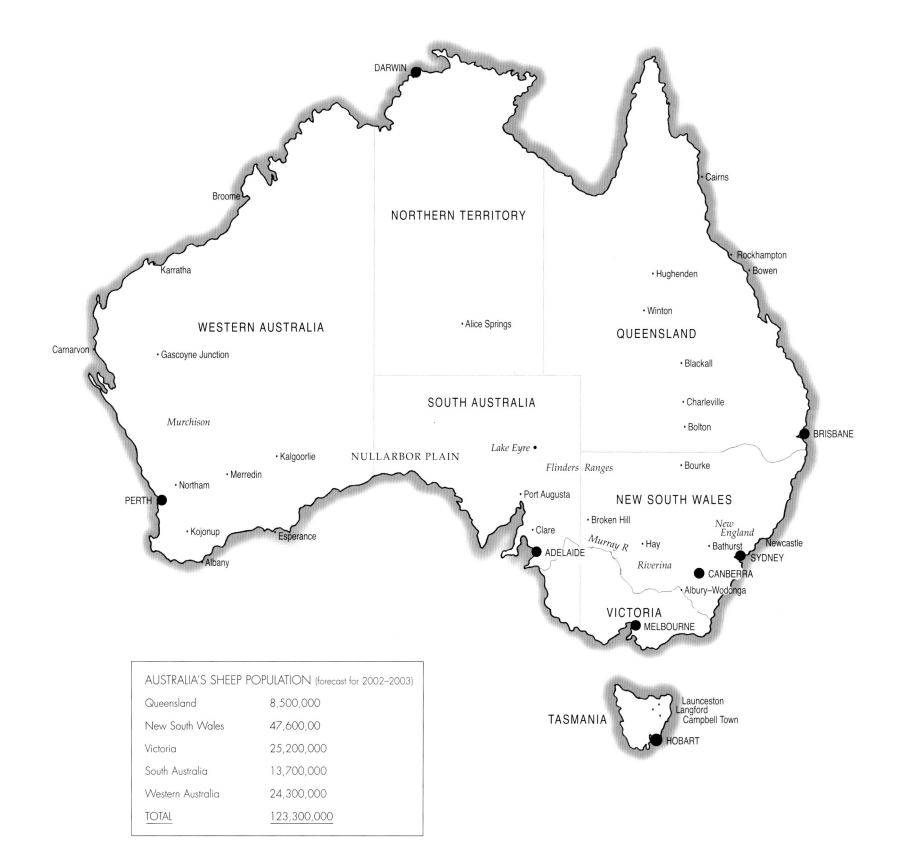

DARWIN

NORTHERN TERRITORY

· Cairns

Broome

· Rockhampton
· Bowen

Karratha

· Hughenden

WESTERN AUSTRALIA

· Alice Springs

QUEENSLAND

Carnarvon

· Winton

· Gascoyne Junction

· Blackall

SOUTH AUSTRALIA

· Charleville

Murchison

· Bolton

BRISBANE

Lake Eyre ·

· Kalgoorlie

NULLARBOR PLAIN

· Bourke

· Merredin

Flinders Ranges

· Northam

NEW SOUTH WALES

PERTH

· Port Augusta

· Broken Hill

*New
England*

· Kojonup

· Clare

Murray R

· Hay

· Bathurst

Newcastle

Esperance

ADELAIDE

Riverina

SYDNEY

Albany

CANBERRA

Albury–Wodonga

VICTORIA

MELBOURNE

Launceston
Langford
Campbell Town

TASMANIA

HOBART

AUSTRALIA'S SHEEP POPULATION (forecast for 2002–2003)	
Queensland	8,500,000
New South Wales	47,600,00
Victoria	25,200,000
South Australia	13,700,000
Western Australia	24,300,000
TOTAL	123,300,000

PREFACE

When discussing the process of writing, Roger McDonald stated recently: 'You must imagine ahead of what you know ... you're actually creating ahead of your own experience ... I think we do imagine our lives as we live them. We decide where it is we are going to go next, and that's imaginative.'

McDonald could also have been writing about the role of the wool industry in our national development, for the imaginative thinkers in that industry laid the path for the unfolding of our national story. But Australia no longer rides on the sheep's back. Its 'imaginers' no longer determine our national direction and destiny. And that is why this is a significant book, for it portrays an industry at a fulcrum moment in its history: a moment when, from the perspective of the present, one looks back on the past knowing that ten years hence things will be radically different, and possibly unrecognisable.

This book is one of those rare amalgams of leading writers and outstanding photographer, and the unexpected marriage of craft in this book has spawned an insightful synergy. Roger McDonald has taken a brisk canter across the early landscape of Australian history — but with the keen and practiced eye of a stockman that misses nothing. Utilising his rural experience, his essay serves as a frame to the wonderful photographic tapestry woven by Richard Woldendorp, and is complemented by the meticulously researched and careful writing of Amanda Burdon. Burdon has brought her considerable experience in editing, honed in the rigorous stylistic milieu of Australian Geographic, to add a third dimension to telling this story about the Australian wool industry. In the process she contributes a comprehensive historical and contemporary perspective.

But it is the imaginative and creative eye behind Richard Woldendorp's photographs that elevates the book to a higher status. Like many great artists, Woldendorp can force us to look at the world afresh. Max Dupain, that icon of early 20th century Australian photography, has said of Woldendorp that he has made 'a one-man Herculean effort to show Australia to the Australians.' Woldendorp does that for the Australian wool industry with his remarkable photographs in this book.

What this combination of craftspeople in pen and shutter have done then is to not only capture the human, animal and resource elements in our national and wool story, but to also depict one of its most fundamental features: that the present day industry is indivisible from its past.

Wherever we go in our wool landscape, history confronts us: sometimes obvious, other times invisible. The merino sheep itself is a thousand-year story writ large in DNA by the hand of man; the landscape is hundreds of millions, even billions of years old; you can bump into shepherd folds from the 1830s, and work in a traditional factory — a shearing shed — whose rituals, process and structures are of the nineteenth century; or you can roll a wool bale whose shape may have been designed for inland camel transport in the 1860s. It is an anachronistic industry, with this juxtaposition of past and present, where deeply embedded ancient practices and tradition clash and blend with the cutting-edge and futuristic new.

Following decades of statutory intervention and divorce from the customer, a senescent wool industry had begun to flounder, overtaken by aggressive competitors; by new consumer generations whose discretionary purchasing power is more likely to focus on electronics and entertainment than a woolly wardrobe; and by alternate, more remunerative land-uses. The upshot is that as we enter a new millenium, within a little over a decade the once mighty Australian wool clip has been slashed in half.

Individuals within the industry are fighting back, however, seeking innovative and alternative directions.

The wool industry has crossed major watersheds in its past. It now stands at perhaps its greatest. But wherever it may reside ten years hence, we will always have this particular fulcrum moment captured through the skills of the artists in this book.

Charles Massy
'Severn Park', Cooma.
8th July, 2002

SHEEP CAME TOO

HOW AUSTRALIA IN THE FIRST ONE HUNDRED YEARS
FOLLOWED IN THEIR TRACKS

BY ROGER MCDONALD

At the end of the eighteenth century, when Botany Bay was settled with convicts and rebels, nobody in the Colonial Office imagined Australia would expand into the greatest wool-producing country on earth.

But sheep came too, peering cautiously out of rough stalls below decks. They staggered ashore with a yearning for open spaces not bred out of them, smelling the dust of sheep country before anyone realised that's what it was. And before too long a national identity gathered around them; the country followed in their tracks.

The earliest arrivals were South African fat-tails, loaded at Cape Town in 1787 and carried by the First Fleet to Botany Bay where they died on landing or were eaten.

More of these odd-looking animals with tails like hairy cricket bats were carried on supply ships that followed — as prison food and garrison food — and suffered a similar unlucky fate except for a handful of animals that survived and interbred.

The scrappy beginnings of a national flock staggered around the huts of Sydney Cove, avoiding the butcher's hook and the spears of the Eora people of Port Jackson but never for long. Their sole purpose was the supply of mutton and just as well, for their wool was rough and poor, mixed with strong frizzled hair and in every variety of colour.

With starvation facing the penal settlement, ships were dispatched to nearby corners of the globe to perform the function of a Noah's Ark.

Bent over his charge and exposed to the elements, a shearer shows how blade shearing was done in the early days. Unlike his modern-day counterpart, who is confined by a machine to one position on the board, the blade shearer could move freely around his charge. The benefit of mechanical shears was not that they were faster — in fact it took some time for shearers to become proficient in their use — but that they took the wool off closer to the sheep's skin, thereby improving yields. Station owners thought that the mechanical shears would enable them to employ unskilled labour, and thus bring down the cost of shearing, but shearing has remained highly specialised.

In 1793 the *Shah Hormuzear* sailed from Calcutta for Botany Bay with one bull, twenty-four cows, 220 Bengal sheep (a wiry-fleeced, small-framed but fertile breed), 130 goats, five horses, six asses, and a cargo of salt beef, sugar, wheat, rice and other grains, plus one cask of cognac brandy, three pipes of Madeira wine and twenty-five reams of Portuguese liquor. The ship came into port at the start of 1794 with half the sheep dead and four horses, three asses, and a few goats surviving.

By mid 1794 the prison colony's flock had increased to a closely shepherded 526. They were pastured on what was available within the limits of settlement — the  swampy lands of the Sydney basin where footrot, liver fluke and stomach worms flourished. The disadvantages, however, were not yet obvious. To newcomers' eyes the country looked like open parkland — perfect for sheep. Few appreciated that Aboriginal burning at intervals had kept it that way, even when within a few years of settlement forests grew up between Parramatta and Emu Plains, in places almost impenetrable.

The main game was mutton, worth thirty or forty times the price of wool. (A ratio that was to move back and forth: by the late 1830s wool peaked at two shillings a pound and mutton could be had for fourpence a pound.) There was potentially more and better land to expand the grazing and perhaps an inland sea or who knew what west of Sydney, beyond the dissected plateau of the Blue Mountains. But white men in those first decades, unless they were escaped convicts with no reason to return, found no way through the maze of sandstone gullies.

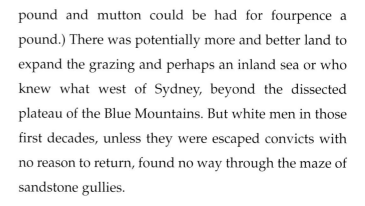

One of the early arrivals at Sydney Cove was Captain John Macarthur, an officer of the New South Wales Corps with an eye to setting himself up with a more extensive land grant than most. He obtained Bengal sheep and crossed them with a young ram, probably of a broad-wool Lincoln-derived breed (principally a meat sheep), which he purchased from the captain of an Irish convict transport in 1794.

Within a short time Macarthur, as he wrote, 'had the satisfaction to see the lambs of the Indian ewes bear a mingled fleece of hair and wool.' A noisy self-publicist, Macarthur later claimed this as a Eureka moment — marking the birth of the fine wool industry of New South Wales. He confidently predicted it would not be a labour-intensive industry, but in a southern district

Early shearing facilities were crude and informal. Sheep flocks were small and shearing was usually conducted out in the open. The first shearing sheds were sometimes little more than simple post and slab-wall shacks topped with a bark roof. Earth floors were later covered with branch mats, fabric and sawn planks and in time, as the size of both flocks and shearing teams grew, the sheds became more permanent.

It was once customary to take a formal photograph of the assembled shearers before the weeks of hard yakka began in a shed — this team was immortalised at Canowie, in southern South Australia, in about 1870. The size of the team reflected the size of the flock and shearers would walk or ride for miles in the hope of securing work. They knew from past experience or word of mouth when and where shearing was taking place and often wrote ahead to secure a stand, enclosing a sovereign as a show of faith. Bicycles were a cheap, light and reliable form of transport in the backblocks. Shearers commonly rode 2000 kilometres in a single season and were known to rack up 5000 kilometres in a year. When they arrived at a station the owner would select his team and 'bush' those he rejected; the chosen ones camping either by the creek or claiming a bunk in the shearers' hut. But despite the relatively primitive living and working conditions shearers were regarded as comparatively well paid. A good shearer could make £3–4 a week in the mid-1880s — the equivalent of what a shepherd earned in two months. Historian Geoffrey Blainey described them as 'the princes of labour'.

not many years later just twenty squatters needed 400 people between them to get the job done.

It would be fifty years before a willing English market was established for New South Wales wool, and many more years before the breeding mix was appropriate across Australia's many contrasting environments (a process of adjustment, as every wool-grower knows, that is still going on). The climate ranged, as a nineteenth century sheep-classer observed, from that of Africa to that of the north of Scotland, with pasture varying from the Syrian desert to an English meadow.

Domesticated sheep were the product of a long line of skilled and perceptive breeders. It was said that not one man in a thousand had accuracy of eye and judgement sufficient to become an eminent breeder. In the Middle East and North Africa the fleece colour of wild sheep had been changed by many generations of herdsmen to white, the hairs to wool, and the fleece selected for continuous growth rather than moulting. It was the creation of the modern, fine wool, shearable sheep. To Charles Darwin, investigating evolution in the mid-nineteenth century, the story was exciting and even romantic, firing his imagination in a way that changed people's view of the world.

It seemed to Darwin as if some unsung genius had chalked out upon a wall a form perfect in itself, and then given it existence. The work of sheep breeders gave him a clue to interpreting natural selection. He noted that in Saxony the importance of selection was so fully recognised that men followed it as a trade. The sheep were placed on a table and studied, like a picture by a connoisseur; this was done three times at intervals of months, and the sheep each time marked and classed, so that the vey best might ultimately be selected for breeding.

The wool industry in Australia, when it developed, would need a sheep not just able to survive, indeed to flourish in a dry, harsh climate on natural herbage, but also able to grow wool of improvable quality and intensifiable fleece density. It would also need breeders of judgement working with a responsive organism.

Sheep are coaxed through a wooden chute in the Edward River to wash their fleeces before shearing in the Riverina. This was a common sight in Australia, where settlement was clustered around river frontages. It prevented shearing blades being dulled by contaminants in the fleece, saved pastoralists money in freight and most of all met buyers' demand for clean wool. When such chutes couldn't be erected, labourers stood up to their waists in water all day to shepherd sheep through billabongs and creeks, or scrubbed the animals one at a time in large tubs filled with soapy water. Sheep washing was largely discontinued when pastoralists spread further inland, away from dependable water sources; when transport improved (riverboats and rail), and market changes meant the premium for scoured wool was no longer paid.

Wool bales were bulky and heavy and the means of transporting them varied with the terrain, the times and the availability and cost of stock. Early bullock transport was slow but reliable, camels trod the more isolated, sandy country and mules and donkeys (top) were even employed in some parts before horse-drawn wagons rose to prominence.

Two impressive bullock teams (bottom) begin the long march to market with the 1908 wool-clip from Mt Gipps station, in far north-western New South Wales. Bullocks provided the first and most enduring form of transport to isolated settlers, especially in the black-soil country. Most squatters employed a bullocky and had at least one team of working bullocks. The first bullock drays had two wheels and could carry about twenty wool bales (two tonnes in today's language), but easily tipped ascending a steep rise. They were superseded by four-wheeled wagons capable of carrying seven tonnes. But travel remained slow — about sixteen plodding kilometres a day — and was often treacherous on roads that were little more than beaten tracks.

One such animal of remarkable hardiness had been selected over many centuries by a North African Berber tribe, the Beni Merines, who had penetrated into Spain as far as Madrid in the thirteenth century. The merino, as the breed was called by the Spanish, was most preciously valued: an animal able to walk long distances, forage in tough going, reproduce and survive in climatic extremes and perhaps even resist internal worms.

This would be a sheep for Australia when it was located, greasy of fleece with a black tipped appearance called 'gum' and 'jar' by English farmers, with a wrinkled neck both prized and despised, and having wool of fineness with density capable of

improvement when crossed with larger-framed animals. Although merinos had been guarded as national treasures by Spain's rulers they had, over time, found their way to studs in Silesia and Saxony, and by the late eighteenth century arrived in France and England where King George III himself pastured a prized flock. After the chaos of the Napoleonic wars in Spain, many more merino sheep would be shipped to England as war booty but they were often allowed to die once landed, under-rated for their folded skin and meatless frames except by discerning breeders.

Merinos had already made an unheralded Australian arrival in a diluted coarse-wool form the year before Macarthur's first purchase. This occurred when at least one ram and a few ewes of Spanish stock were shipped from the Spanish mission at Monterey, California, as a result of Captain George Vancouver's six-year world voyage of discovery. Chance soon intervened with another and stronger contribution to merino presence when the Dutch commandant at Cape Town committed suicide. His flock of Spanish merinos was purchased from his widow by a ship's captain sent from the prison colony for livestock and provisions. On his return to Australia Captain Waterhouse sold the few merinos that survived to a handful of keen buyers including John Macarthur and the Reverend Samuel Marsden (who interested himself in livestock when not improving convict morals with Christianity and the lash). Macarthur paid up to £16 each for three other Spanish imports, a very large sum for the times and an indication of the money-making potency of owning domesticated animals in a place where only weird marsupials, venomous reptiles, and strange screeching birds utilised the pastures and offered no profit.

The Aborigines for their part were seen as wandering people without special attachment to defined acreages

A water-borne wool team crosses the Murray River at Echuca, in northern Victoria, on one of the early punts. Town founder Henry Hopwood and enterprising cattleman James 'Jimmy' Maiden installed the first narrow punts across the river near present-day Moama in the 1840s, paving the way for transport to Melbourne, from where the wool-clip was shipped to Sydney. Previously the region's wool had to make the arduous journey to Sydney by bullock wagon.

who might at best be made into useful herders if only they could be cured of their habit of spearing sheep and attacking shepherds. A gift of hunting dogs from the farmhouse and the use of offal when an animal was killed, as well as a share of milk from the cows was received with almost overwhelming gratitude — not surprisingly, since the hardscrabble of hunting and gathering was miraculously eased by such trifling peace offerings. Aboriginal women proved remarkable blade shearers with a gift of calming sheep no European shearer was able to equal, and both men and women shepherded, mustered, yarded, penned-up, piece-picked and cleaned, on places where they had been born, in some areas through until the 1930s. As a

schoolboy in Bourke in the early 1950s I remember my Aboriginal friends disappearing from the classroom for weeks indeed months on end when it came time to go picking up in the sheds and scouring the paddocks for the little bit extra that could be made from dead wool.

Yet as one historian of the industry has said, when fuelled by the drive for profits, the fierce trio of lust, adventure and greed were almost unstoppable. No matter how kindly and peaceably inclined individual settlers strove to be (such as the Hentys of Western Victoria and the Archers of Central Queensland), by their very occupation of country newcomers made trouble with Aborigines inevitable, even though they avoided murder themselves. Wherever the sheep frontier extended over the next sixty or seventy years a sequence of attack, counter-attack, outrage and vengeance followed. Pioneer pastoralist Niel Black of Western Victoria confided in a private letter to his business partner in England, that in some places new-comers were advised to make a purchase only after so many natives had been killed that little trouble could be expected.

By 1800 there were 6,000 sheep in the vicinity of Sydney; five years later there were 20,000 hammering the feed on the narrow Cumberland plain where within another decade the natural grasses were eaten out and caterpillar plagues were endemic. It was a mixed mob including the Cape, Bengal, Californian Spanish and Irish varieties, as well as Southdowns, Teeswaters, and possibly Leicesters and Lincolns — broad woolled meat sheep, yet with enough merino from various other arrivals to show the potential of cross-breeding.

By the turn of the century, 180,000 sheep were being shorn annually at Belltrees, one of the premier sheep stations in the undulating upper Hunter of New South Wales. The shed employed forty-two blade shearers for five months of the year. Some of the best wool was grown in the upper reaches of the estate, at an adjoining property called Ellerston, and it was easier to walk the sheep thirty-two kilometres to the shearing shed, involving fifteen sometimes hazardous Hunter River crossings, than to risk the wool wagon getting bogged. A single sheep suspension bridge built by the station's blacksmith helped expedite this mob's passage in 1901.

Mounted police and military troops (top) descend on Barcaldine, in western Queensland, at the height of the Great Shearers' Strike in 1891. This violent and protracted industrial dispute engulfed much of the state for six months and tested the strength of the fledgling Amalgamated Shearers' Union, formed in 1886 — the precursor of the Australian Workers' Union (1894), from which evolved the Australian Labor Party. Shearers downed tools over what they considered appalling pay and working conditions, and the pastoralists' use of 'scab' labour. Thousands of shearers locked out of sheds set up a shanty camp outside Barcaldine. During the height of the strike eight Queensland woolsheds were burnt down, sheep were slaughtered, fences cut and physical violence ensued. With its shearers close to starvation, the union finally relented and permitted its members to work alongside the non-union labour, however the strike established the ASU as a strong negotiator and from then on shearing conditions steadily improved.

The riverboat era dawned shortly after 1853, when the *Lady Augusta* carried the first cargo of wool bales from Swan Hill in Victoria to Goolwa in South Australia, and soon revolutionised wool transport. At its peak, between 1860 and 1910, hundreds of riverboats plied the Murray, Darling and Murrumbidgee rivers and their tributaries towing capacious barges like this one at Echuca wharf (bottom). Welcoming as many as 240 paddle-steamers in a season, Echuca was the largest inland port in Australia and in 1880 handled wool worth £2.5 million.

When samples of eight fleeces were sent to England in 1800 little of that promise was evident. The wool was declared suitable for cattle bedding, brick mortar, road making, mattress stuffing, and for throwing away. When Macarthur was exiled to England for nine years following a vicious feud with Governor Bligh, his wife Elizabeth brilliantly performed the role of studmaster. When Macarthur showed one of their Cape merino fleeces to the king's wool-classer it drew high praise: 'Quite free from hair, and an excellent quality; could the colony produce such kinds of wools it would be a great acquisition to our manufactory in England.'

Thus endorsed, Macarthur returned to Australia but not before expanding his land grant in the area called the Cowpastures (later called Camden), south-west of Sydney, and buying seven rams and three ewes at the first public sale of George III's Spanish merinos. The average price was £15 per head and cheap at the price. They were the first authenticated pure Spanish merino sheep brought to Australia.

Despite his key purchases and his acreages eventually expanding to 60,000, Macarthur was not as responsive to local conditions as the Rev Samuel Marsden, who on his farm at Parramatta embarked on breeding a sheep calculated for the country rather than chasing purity and fineness. 'The main object I have constantly kept in view,' wrote Marsden in 1805, 'has been to improve the constitution of the sheep, the weight in their carcases, and quality of the wool. I have not always chosen a ram with the finest fleece.' It was the direction of the future, but did not mean the smooth rise of Rev Marsden's flock. By the mid-1820s his use of

Southdowns on a hairy Cape and Bengal base had degraded his wool and he obtained Saxon rams to bring it back, with the result that very quickly, by the end of that decade, he was yielding well once more and getting letters of praise from London wool-dealers. In 1825 Alexander Riley, a former merchant, landed a flock of superbly coddled Saxon merinos, said to be each like a woolly pasha in its own padded pen. He grazed then at Cavan, near Yass. By 1838 when Marsden died, his and Riley's were two of the key flocks of the colony, and their bloodlines persist to this day. The number of sheep in New South Wales by then reached almost 1,500,000.

Macarthur's obsession with ultrafine wool certainly played its part in putting low microns into the mix of Australian breeds, but it did so at the expense of environmental factors. His genetically guarded flock would end its days as a small-framed, low-cutting, exquisitely fleeced historical curiosity. The greatness of the merino was to be its hardiness and versatility, not its purity alone.

The word versatile might also be used of the workforce demanded by sheep — following in their tracks — true Australians as some were now beginning to call themselves as the nineteenth century took hold, those once-reluctant arrivals bearing manacle scars on their wrists and ankles, a tough and desperate ex-convict crew available for shepherding.

In 1813 the Blue Mountains were crossed and the slopes and plains of New South Wales were opened to livestock. The whole population, poor and rich, was bent on acquiring wealth; the subject of wool and sheep grazing was an incessant topic of conversation. Officialdom became alarmed. Concern was expressed that sheep plus unlimited land would turn the colony into a horde of wanderers living on milk and flesh, and getting drunk on fermented mare's milk. So by government decree settlement was restricted to what were called the Nineteen Counties, whose borders stretched up the Hunter Valley to the north, as far as the Bathurst region to the west, and not much past Goulburn to the south (where the nearby Canberra region provided such good grazing that when the national capital was founded one hundred years later it was commonly referred to as a fine sheep station ruined).

Anyone who grazed outside the limit of settlement was nicknamed a squatter — a taker of unclaimed land without title. The first half of the nineteenth century belonged to the squatter and shepherd; the second half to the shearer and pastoralist. It would be disorder turned into organisation: unfenced to fenced; hard labour to labour politics; colonial to federal statehood. All in the sheep's tracks.

Squatters occupied the waterholes, river frontages and billabongs. They scorned the unwatered acreages at their backs except for grazing them — because they knew that if, in the end, land laws were twisted in their favour, they would get them cheap anyway. They were right. Governors threw up their hands and exclaimed they might as well attempt to confine the Arabs of the Desert within a circle as hold the squatters to the Nineteen Counties.

From illegal beginnings the word squatter very quickly became something of a class word, indicating wealth and power. It took less than a generation for determined men of shady background to become landed gentry with stations on the creek and mansions in Potts Point or South Yarra. By the middle of the century it was suggested by the dignitary WC Wentworth that a colonial peerage be established for these Shepherd Kings. It didn't work out as a way to cloak their rough origins, but the word squattocracy took hold, half mocking, half respectful — a fairly Australian state of affairs.

The advent of the motor vehicle, typified by this early truck laden with wool bales at Mudgee, greatly improved transport options for wool producers. The advantages were supreme over horse and bullock and the old ways were consigned to the museum almost overnight. Author HM Barker comments on the revolution in *Camels and the Outback*: 'When motor lorries reached the back country and began to displace camels, it gave us an awful shock. After being accustomed to taking a load of wool to the railway or port say, 100 miles away and bringing a load of general cargo back, taking fourteen days for the round trip, we could not believe that it could be done, and done easily, with a motor in one day … What was quite unexpected was the way even the most conservative of station owners took to motors readily. Some had defied every modern invention, such as machine shearing, all their lives; yet they took to motors straight away.' These days woolgrowers mostly rely on Australia's extensive road network and a fleet of sophisticated semi-trailers to ferry their wool to market.

The New South Wales slopes and plains were too far out for the immediate mutton market but wool had the virtue of being imperishable and would be as fresh in England as under a gum tree. In the 1820s a sheep-run with its home paddock near Lithgow had shepherds ranging as far north-west as the Warrumbungle ranges. The sheep were walked all the way back to the home station for washing and shearing, saving freight by carrying their own wool. By late that decade there were 80,000 sheep in the Hunter Valley alone, and in 1826 the million pound mark (by weight) was reached with Australian wool exports to England. However the fleece was coarse compared with the best Spanish and Saxon imports from Continental flocks, and the word Australia was not highly regarded in a wool market showing a marked trend towards worsted, a cloth requiring longer and increasingly finer and better wools. There was also the growing competition of cottons against woollens cutting in.

Growers did not yet feel the intense pressure on quality that emerged in the post-goldrush decades (the 1850s onwards) when wool pushed ahead of meat as the basis of sheep industry profit, and cattle took second place to sheep on the saltbush plains. Nor did they get the reward in prices either. But all the same, market feedback shaped work practices as well as wool types. After all, wool was the only export we had, apart from whaling and sealing, collectively known as the fisheries.

Sheep washing began as a farming practice when fleece shorn in the grease and bundled any old how were declared unacceptable by London firms in the 1820s and woolgrowers were urged to wash their flocks clean of soil and impurities before shearing. The need to pack shepherded sheep into portable yards or hurdles each night increased the dirt they collected and added to worm and fluke infection, for which there were no effective drenches, only a variety of questionable cures based on tobacco, kerosene, bluestone and the like. Much country, though suited to sheep, was degraded to either loose or hard-panned dirt by severe grazing on thin pasture and so compounded both handling and environmental problems. Sheep country, as yet unfenced, became a spread of muddy waterholes and stirred-up creeks and rivers, necessitating ingenious penning systems be developed for the wool wash.

The washing itself was done by the shearers, who demanded lashings of rum to get through work that required standing in water for hours at a time, over

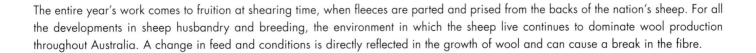

The entire year's work comes to fruition at shearing time, when fleeces are parted and prised from the backs of the nation's sheep. For all the developments in sheep husbandry and breeding, the environment in which the sheep live continues to dominate wool production throughout Australia. A change in feed and conditions is directly reflected in the growth of wool and can cause a break in the fibre.

Resembling a snowy blanket, clean wool is spread out to dry naturally at the Garmouth station wool scour in New South Wales (top). Large-scale scouring, during which wool was soaked in big vats of soapy water, then rinsed and dried, was most common in northern New South Wales and Queensland, where the majority of the country's fifty-two steam-powered public wool scours were built to take advantage of river frontage (bottom) and artesian or bore waters. Scouring was initially assigned to shearers but in time labourers, including Aboriginal women, were seconded. Once the wool was washed it was spread thinly on the ground to dry and repeatedly turned by hand — an extremely tedious and risky process, especially in winter. From the 1880s onwards manufacturers conceded that outback scouring had its limitations and most of the wool-clip was sold in the grease, then industrially scoured.

many days. Each property had its own agreement with workers in an atmosphere in which employer attitudes were shaped by having traditionally had convict labour on their own terms. Dawn to dark would remain the work-hours rule until late in the nineteenth century, with the Saturday finish at four if workers were lucky. With rampant epidemics of scab, a skin disease unknown in today's flocks involving the fleece eventually falling off, washing was even more unpleasant, and sometimes useless if clips were baled blackened by the scratching and rubbing of scab-infected sheep. Little wonder 'scab' came to mean union traitor. The build-up of tension between employer and worker that was to give birth to the union movement in the next half century can be easily imagined in such a breeding ground of resentment and exploitation. Yet the atmosphere in a blade shearing shed was relatively peaceable — apart from bleating sheep, the curses of men and the call for tar. With men taking up their shearing positions wherever they chose, it looked more relaxed than today's noisy situation.

The long tradition of excluding women from the sheds rests on the fact that, quite simply, there were few to no women at station headquarters, a fact often noted by travellers and a state of affairs that lasted until graziers broke the habit of living in town and established family life in the bush. Charles Darwin commented on this situation when he visited the Bathurst district in 1836:

> Although the farm is well stocked with every requisite, there was an apparent absence of comfort; & not even one woman resided here. — The Sunset of a fine day will generally cast an air of happy contentment on any scene; but here at this retired farmhouse the brightest tints on the surrounding woods could not make me forget that forty hardened profligate men were ceasing from their daily labours, like the Slaves from Africa, yet without their just claim for compassion.

One of the contradictions of the industry at the shed level, however, was and remains the love of the day's routine on the board, that small arena resembling a theatrical stage with its time structure of several acts and intervals of smokos and dinner break. Everything was fought out there in the contest to fill the bale. The work was unrelenting, exacting and somewhat exhausting, eventually crippling, but the spirit of comradeship and rivalry prevailed and lifted the labour beyond the ordinary industrial moment of drudgery and repetition for worker and woolgrower alike.

Use of blade shears was not always accompanied by the sound of clacking metal, as finely sharpened shears could sometimes be carved with an almost hushed whisper through the cleaner wools. But the work was still arduous and shearing was the crux of the industry, as it still is, the moment when woolgrowers agonise in a plight of dependence over whether they have the right team — there on time, pulling together, and skilled enough — for the sheep they've been nurturing for years.

From the earliest days shearers emerged as a potential power in the land, and started a habit of working themselves into exhaustion and drinking themselves into delirium, just to worry the woolgrower more over whether they'd turn up the next day. Indeed the practice of drinking the cheque became standard practice among rural workers, except perhaps for a few puritanical types, often Scots, a variation on the rum-soaked rite of convict experience. It was a process of killing the pain, coping with the realities of climate, isolation, exploitation and punishment. The boozing went on into the night in the workers' camp, while on the other side of the gully the squatters or swells would also go at it all night when they chose. But they were more self-righteous about their carousing, on occasion offering the excuse there was nowhere for their visitors to sleep, and everyone had to be awake to set off at daybreak for a communal muster or a hunt with kangaroo dogs.

After shearing, wool was sorted, usually into no more than two classes. As time went on the rough lever woolpress was replaced by the screw press, which gained growers a discount of a farthing a pound for the preferred transportation by bullock cart. Dockside woolstores pressed the bale into half that size by hydraulic apparatus, and then on board ship a dozen or more men reduced it even further, so that by the time the ship sailed the wool was four times more compressed than when it began up country.

Just when the physical barriers to inland regions opened wide the country went into drought. The fact that the best wool-sheep country in the world was in a drought-prone tract of the southern hemisphere was both a blessing and a curse. Not that anything like an El Nino effect was recognised in that or the next century either — only an oft-expressed wish for the seasons to come good, as if the proper pattern was plenty and everything else real about this country just an aberration.

The blessing, though, that remained, was that sheep thrived on natural herbage adapted to hard conditions, such as varieties of saltbush in the country farther out. Overstocking meant stripping the haystack of native foliage, but what was overstocking? Nobody knew without experience, and besides, human psychology lived on hope as much as on greed.

Sheep munched Australia bare through the nineteenth century, a process hastened by the introduction of rabbits in the late 1850s and the proliferation of other fast-breeding domesticated stock running wild — goats, horses, camels, donkeys, Javanese buffalo — to name just a few, who were escorted by flights of smaller companions — sparrows, starlings and mynah birds. The whole pestilential parade travelled through a landscape that sometimes seemed composed of nothing but introduced weeds devised as special

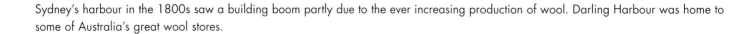

Sydney's harbour in the 1800s saw a building boom partly due to the ever increasing production of wool. Darling Harbour was home to some of Australia's great wool stores.

tortures in each particular region where they adaptively thrived — burrs of all shapes and hardness, thorns, wiry grasses, and soft and attractive foliage of species either poisonous to stock or digestively unusable. Then there were the virtual Plagues of Egypt afflicting sheep as the century progressed: scab, footrot, and catarrh. Fly-strike may seem to be the ubiquitous one but it only emerged around 1901, the date of Federation.

Some things about sheep had to be lucky — those creatures easier to be loved in general than liked in particular. An Australian poet who was also a grazier resorted to blasphemy and demanded to know, 'What cynic godhead made them?' Banjo Paterson, who grew up on Illalong Station near Yass, and whose son Hugh  spent his life managing sheep properties, was speaking from experience when he wrote: 'merinos made our men sardonic or they wept.'

The curtain-raiser drought between 1813 and 1816 left 5,000 sheep and 3,000 cattle dead in the Sydney region, and between 1826 and 1829 the cycle struck again. In the meantime the golden fleece continued to entice. At least 5,000 merinos entered New South Wales between 1821 and 1831, and over 1,500 reached Van Diemen's Land in the same period. Then again drought struck

for three years in the mid 1830s, and again in the 1840s, weeding out many poor managers and killing off breed variations ill-adapted to the cycle. Prayers for rain dried the throats of preachers, and governors declared days of thanksgiving when drought broke.

Stud sheep importation from Europe continued whatever the conditions dealt. It was an amazing effort of trying something out in a process that gathered pace. By good luck, experimental management and long-distance travel involving extended buying expe-  ditions to the source of bloodlines in Europe (France, Saxony, Silesia), the best fine-wool merinos in the world formed the base of most early stud flocks during those hard yet expansionist times. Letters written in the age of sail give the impression that trips back and forth across the world looking for stock, sometimes of two or more years duration, were as easy as jaunts by passenger jet. This was not so. Members of almost every pioneer family seem to have been shipwrecked or drowned at some time or other.

In New South Wales, with its vast amount of country thrown open, increase of stock numbers took precedence over sheep improvement. But in Van Diemen's Land it was a different story. Finer sheep were bred, in part assisted by a pedigree flock moved from Norfolk

The interior of the Wooloomooloo wool store showing conveyor belts which were highly innovative at the time of construction. The building has recently been transformed into hotel and unit accommodation.

Island when the penal settlement was closed. The Midlands of Van Diemen's Land effectively became a stud operation in the 1820s and 30s, assisted by a plentiful supply of convict shepherds and safeguarded from Aboriginal attack by the pitiless policy of rounding up those left. Anger against the Tasmanians was redoubled because they took fondly to sheep dogs, which the settlers themselves had brought into the dingoless environment and passed on as gifts. Of course these dogs savaged sheep and the people were blamed.

In the Midlands with its richer pasture and smaller paddock size breeders were able to experiment with fencing long before it was possible in the rest of Australia. The Midlands became the second main focus of quality sheep breeding after the Macarthurs' Camden–Liverpool area (now part of expanded urban Sydney). To follow in importance would be Western Victoria, in a strip of country north of Warrnambool, and then the Riverina north of Deniliquin, which would, in time, supply the country with its most dominant and successful strain of wool-bearing sheep, the Peppin merino.

Word of expansive sheep country roused considerable interest in Britain. It was a time of big and sometimes rash colonial investment. Certain success stories soon entered legend. The Henty family of Sussex, owners of one of England's best flocks bred from George III's Spanish merinos, sailed across the world, first to the Swan River (where the poor soil beat them), then to Van Diemen's Land with their studmasters, shepherds, servants and sheep all travelling together. It was 1831 and it had just become harder to acquire large tracts of land, due to a sudden change of policy. The privatisation of crown land now involved selling to the highest bidder in the convict colony. So the Hentys almost immediately looked across the Bass Strait to the opposite coast, the terra incognita of the Port Phillip district of New South Wales where, after a brief crisis of conscience, they squatted. Other families and stock units, including a cluster from Devon, were to follow in this migration of not just stud sheep, but of skilled handlers bringing their store of knowledge and a scorn of government regulation that grew apace the more they tried it on, until it became the established state of affairs.

Between 1831 and 1836 Major Thomas Mitchell, surveyor, literary stylist, and capable explorer, made three expeditions — first to the catchments of the Namoi, Gwydir, Barwon and Darling rivers, then down the Murrumbidgee and Murray. On his third expedition he struck into the part of New South Wales

Hand-sawn timbers stand the test of time in sheep yards still in use today. Farmers fashioned fences and holding paddocks from whatever materials were inexpensive and readily available — from stones and brush to galvanised iron and timber.

eventually to be called Western Victoria and penned lines making inevitable the spectacle of hundreds of thousands of sheep jostling into his wheel tracks barely before the dew was dried from them:

> The land is, in short, open and available in its present state, for all the purposes of civilized men. We traversed it in two directions with heavy carts, meeting no other obstruction than the softness of the rich soil; and in returning over flowery plains and green hills, fanned by the breezes of early spring, I named this region Australia Felix, the better to distinguish it from the parched deserts of the interior country, where we had wandered so unprofitably, and so long.

On this last leg of a considerable hike Mitchell to his astonishment found the Hentys and their merino sheep, land-taking in an unauthorised fashion and coolly composed about it. After recovering from finding people already in residence at Portland Mitchell decided he rather liked their style. The Hentys' named their station after their breed of sheep. A new name for squatters would be 'Pure Merino', signifying the hands-on investor who in a short generation built veritable castles from a chosen breed of fleece and the land underpinning its growth. As had already happened north, west, and south of Sydney, there was a land rush west of Port Phillip preceding the gold rushes of the 1850s.

In this way a market for cast for age sheep from Van Diemen's Land was created almost as soon the stock were ready. Land was available and Tasmanian ewes being discarded near the end of their breeding life might still have another lamb in them. In 1836 as many as 100,000 head were brought over Bass Strait to Port Phillip, which at the time was a settlement of three or four wattle and daub huts, a few turf huts, and about twelve or fifteen tents. Port Phillip was to have, 150 years later, a population of several million and the distinction of being that rare large city of the world surrounded by excellent sheep country — to the extent that the sobriquet 'suburban shearer' was appropriate, as at least 250,000 sheep were shorn by shearers living in Melbourne at the end of the 1980s.

While the drover with his horses, dogs, and cook's turnout travels through Australian lore and legend, incessantly moving stock from one end of the occupied lands to the other, it is easily forgotten that vast numbers of sheep were carried around the Australian colonies — and later the states of the

---

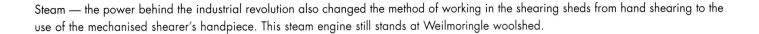

Steam — the power behind the industrial revolution also changed the method of working in the shearing sheds from hand shearing to the use of the mechanised shearer's handpiece. This steam engine still stands at Weilmoringle woolshed.

Slow steam tractor-driven wagons (top), fired by coal or wood, sometimes served as feeders to the railways, which were capable of carrying far greater loads further and faster — this one (bottom) steaming into the port of Darling Harbour. At first colonial traders greeted woolgrowers on the outskirts of town to broker a deal or the growers shipped their wool direct to England themselves in the fast wool clippers. Then came the wool consignment agencies, wool brokers the likes of Thomas Mort and Richard Goldsbrough, and, in the 1850s, colonial merchants and importing houses. By the late 1880s many of the bullocks and horses so long employed to transport wool were only taking clips to the nearest railway or river steamer for dispatch to the large wool houses at major ports.

Commonwealth — by ship. Stock voyages to Queensland and Western Australia were to become routine. It was the chosen method, rather than droving, for at least one selected flock which travelled from the southern Riverina to Adelaide and then on by foot, out into the dry country of the West Darling, north of the Riverina. Records survive of shepherds aboard small sailing ships taking care of their flocks with the dedication of sickroom attendants, creeping about the sheep all day, assisting those that had fallen down, and feeding them with handfuls of hay dipped in water. After all, it was the way sheep had arrived here in the first place: shepherded.

That evocative word shepherd is still used in New Zealand for the sheep-handling property worker (equipped with long crook and accompanied by a far-ranging dog). Its revival this side of the Tasman might perhaps add a depth of understanding to the role of the grazier or station hand on the farm bike in Australia. To shepherd is to understand, to follow, to watch out for, as well as to lead, conduct, direct and guide. What dedicated sheep man or woman does otherwise?

Shepherds were the first whites to confront the realities of a harsh environment on their own as a matter of course, and it is not surprising that those who were not

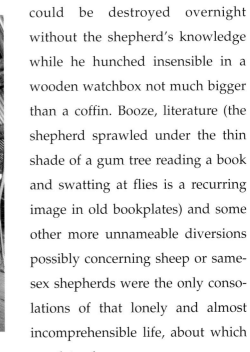

speared by local Aborigines went mad from isolation and drink. It was the work of the footsore, brain-maddened shepherd and his lonely hut-keeper that made the squatter's life possible. It was said that the very easiness of the work maddened men of energy while the unmistakeable sobbing howl of dingoes raised the hair on the shepherd's scalp and made the hut-keeper reach for his carbine. The whole flock could be destroyed overnight without the shepherd's knowledge while he hunched insensible in a wooden watchbox not much bigger than a coffin. Booze, literature (the shepherd sprawled under the thin shade of a gum tree reading a book and swatting at flies is a recurring image in old bookplates) and some other more unnameable diversions possibly concerning sheep or same-sex shepherds were the only consolations of that lonely and almost incomprehensible life, about which a young squatter complained:

> There is a continual scene of dissipation and drinking among the lower orders. And we poor swells instead of partaking in any sort of enjoyment are kept continually galloping from station to station in mortal terror that Long Jim, Lanky Dick, with Bobby the Bull are all drunk, with the sheep looking after themselves on the tops of the mountains.

An 1861, Humble and Nicholson Ferrier's lever press. As well as improving the methods of wool handling, the press became a highly ornate and richly decorated addition to the otherwise rudimentary woolshed.

For decades there were no fences, only brushwood rails in the holding yards, and it was not until almost mid-century that the swing drafting gate and the drafting race were invented. Before that the solution to boxing with neighbouring flocks was grabbing the offending sheep by the hind leg and yanking it out of the mob. The shepherding life, with its forgotten pedigree in Australia, slowly evolved through the decades to the management of larger flocks, upwards of 3,000 to 4,000 per man by around 1860, and the shepherd eventually camping out rather than folding the sheep in portable yards at night.

In this practice called Tim Shea-ing, the sheep wandered and the shepherd followed, and where the sheep settled for the night so did the shepherd. Although no unfenced run was safe from other stock ravaging its feed, and stock losses through wandering sheep being lost were a possibility, with wild dog attack always having its seasons (as it still does), the practice led to healthier flocks. Maybe Tim Shea-ing is why fragments of old iron cooking pots can still be found on long-time sheep camps, places where pigface, horehound and marshmallow proliferate — weeds that shepherds sometimes boiled up to prevent scurvy (Barcoo rot), counteracting their unrelenting diet of mutton.

A shepherding instinct in stud breeders made them appreciate quietness and easy workability in a sheep as well as innumerable other traits of preferred behaviour invisible in today's look-over from the window of an idling Toyota. The best had shepherded in the British Isles in their youth and when they turned to breeding knew what to look for in a sheep destined for a particular habitat. The old Scots shepherds said that what was bred in the bone came out in the flesh.

So began a long process of breeding characteristics into Australian sheep as a tribute to close understanding. This was what the Peppins of Wanganella (originally of Old Shute Farm, Dulverton, Somerset) did when almost beaten by the country north of Deniliquin. They decided to try again and attempt to breed a type of sheep suitable to the Riverina and beyond, a larger, more robust, stronger-woolled sheep and with a bulky back to stand up to summer dust and heat.

By the mid-nineteenth century sheep numbers exceeded fifteen million and were growing at more than ten per cent per year. (The one hundred million mark would be reached by 1900.) West and north of the

Click go the shears was not always the reality when using traditional handpieces. A good shearer with a sharp blade and wool of the right condition could slice through the wool silently.

Great Dividing Range there was hardly anyone now who did not work with sheep or was otherwise connected to them — the shepherd, the sheep-washer, the bladeshearer at the side of big flocks running up into the tens and even hundreds of thousands as sheep-handling skills in the new country increased. There was also the sun-blackened bullocky transporting bales to the dockside; the stock agent in his spotted cravat; the bank manager with his look of an undertaker ready to pounce. Divisions of labour provided a mirror and an impetus to a society in the making.

The Australian colonies shocked and exhilarated new arrivals coming from the old. Foundation as a convict colony infected attitudes to authority unknown in class-strangled England. Individuals who had been flogged and mistreated passed on their bitterness; the press of the day was venomous towards those in charge, and brazenly free of speech. The bitterness was not eased by the squatting rushes which were a violation of land laws framed to benefit the small selector and cynically turned to the advantage of those who already held the best water, best home paddocks, and besides had money in the bank for the time being at least.

Landed or landless, the sheep fed all. Mutton was cheap, plentiful and so common it was considered merely the soil on which wool was grown. Migrants were attracted from England on the promise of meat three times a day, whereas at home it was a scrap of fatty bacon if they were lucky. The average shearer was said to eat around twenty pounds (nine kilograms) of chops and joints per week. It was not the British way to do anything imaginative with meat, and nineteenth-century Australia was a British holding. 'Only in Turkey, I am told, are worse mutton dishes served than on the average Australian sheep station,' wrote the poet John Manifold (who grew up on one). A newly slaughtered killer started a cycle of consumption:

> We had the liver for supper. Excellent! Never tasted anything half so good.
>
> 23rd — Dined on sheep's head and trotters. (Tea to drink, *toujours*.)
>
> 24th — Saddle of mutton.
>
> 25th — Leg.
>
> 26th — Shoulder.
>
> 27th — Leg.
>
> 28th — Shoulder.
>
> 29th — Finished the sheep, and polished the bones.
>
> (EW Landor, Swan River District, 1847)

Assisted immigration grew from the shortage of labour during the squatting boom and new arrivals jumped into a unique social situation. In the structure of work in the sheep yards a society under creation was seen every day in the realm of worker–boss relations. Snobbery was not absent and anyone who believed that Australia was a classless society benefited from a spell in the sheep yards. It was said that those on a higher rung fought to prevent those on the next one down from climbing upwards. But the structure was complicated because in the yards and in the sheds those on supposedly lower rungs turned the whole thing over and put themselves on the top. In other words, here was a country where the worker might be king.

This made Australia a rare old place in New Chum eyes. Winds blew from the wrong direction, the seasons were reversed, and the sun hung in the wrong part of the sky. Hot Christmas pudding was eaten in summer heat. The aristocracy of the working man epitomised by the shearer was noted by all comers.

It worked out though. The traditional hope of emigrants was that where they were going would become the opposite of where they were from. In this they cannot have been disappointed. It was the wool culture in brief and Australia in summary: chance, opportunity, adaptation, setback, and success. We can look into the sheep yards of

today and see the Australia of back then. Wool tells the Australian story whichever way it tumbles.

A word beginning to be heard in all this was 'mateship' — employers had their associations, of which the biggest was government; and so mightn't workers band together too, to make thmselves stronger, and have their voices heard? A mates' parliament? Impossible dream, but then among flocks

dreams seemed to happen, from the lowliest shepherd whittling a stick to pass time watching sheep, to the breeder pursuing images of greatness by imagining sheep, to the shearer cursing them and trying to improve himself by shearing sheep.

When drought struck again, worse than ever, major rivers (such as the Murrumbidgee) dried up, unemployment became rife, and the government found itself in huge debt to pay for its immigration policies. The crash of the 1840s served as an extreme model for the bad times to come over the next century and a half. How bad can be guessed by sheep prices dropping, in an example from New England, from £3 per head to one penny per head. The whole community was horrorstruck, and nothing, it seemed, would avert general bankruptcy. Melbourne, where there had been a speculation boom, was said to be no longer Melbourne (ie., fast, fashionable, spendthrift). No money, no credit, no trade, nothing but failure — the sheriff's officer carrying out repossessions being the only active man in the community. Even the lawyers could scarcely succeed in getting paid.

There followed a solution, somewhat stomach-turning, based on the fact that the major source of

---

In the 1980s some of Melbourne's trams were decorated with the merino, before the downturn in the wool price of the 1990s.

lighting throughout the Empire was the candle, and that a major animal-fat by-product was soap. It was realised that the oversupplied sheep industry had fat on the hoof to spare — sheep worth nothing could be boiled down, or melted down, and their fatty conglomerate product, tallow, could be sold for as much as six shillings per head. It started a boom of boiling vats or tallow houses on the outskirts of every major town, sending a wave of stink over everything. By 1850 over 2.5 million sheep were being melted down annually. Carts loaded with legs of boiled mutton at sixpence each appeared in the streets.

A benefit of the boiling-down was the large-scale reduction in numbers of old and inferior sheep including hairy-coated sheep still carrying fat-tailed Cape and Bengal characteristics. Speculators who had counted numbers of sheep rather than quality were out of the trade. Others turned to cattle until cattle in their turn went bad. Sheep breeders in for the long term began to focus more keenly on the wool side of production, and professional wool-classers from this time onwards had more influence.

The most important of these was the Yorkshire sheep and wool-classer, Thomas Shaw, sent out to Australia in the 1840s as a buyer and sorter and instructor of sorters. There had been something brilliant about Australian fleeces but a severe drop in quality posed a puzzle. Over the the next couple of decades, and succeeded by one of his sons, Shaw made Australia his home and wielded great influence at the stud end. A confirmed alcoholic always carrying a black bag of hefty content, Shaw travelled extensively through the eastern colonies and New Zealand observing climate, soil and working conditions, and noting the casual unselective methods of sheep breeding predominating. At first his judgements sounded close to the sorts of criticisms made of wild colonial boys, not just of wool-bearing hides, and he offended colonial pride by declaring what he saw as a mongrel breed in which was found every shade between the real Australian merino, as he called it, and the dried up Leicester, mixed up with myriads not fit to class as respectable goats.

Shaw eventually settled in the Riverina, hoisting his shingle in the village of Wanganella, in the saltbush country where the Peppins and later FS Falkiner and notably Otway Falkiner were to make their mark. He was to be credited with virtually creating the Australian merino fleece in its best and most recognisable qualities: fine wool with weight and length. He insisted that the woolgrower's cross must be made

An enduring farming icon, the Furphy's Farm Water Cart ascribed to the motto: 'Good — Better — Best, Never Let it Rest, Till Your Good is Better, And Your Better — Best.'

Some observers attribute the design and dimensions of early 310-pound wool bales to camels — two bales fitted neatly either side of the animal's hump — while others contend that the size met the loading requirements of the *Cutty Sark*. Camels (top) were integral to the wool industry in the early days. Hardy and strong, they were common bearers of the wool-clip in Western Australia and the sandy country of South Australia, where the distances to market were greater, the temperatures hotter and the terrain more demanding. Each camel could carry a 440–660-pound burden.

A tower of 150 wool bales, this load (bottom) drawn by a team of draughthorses constituted a record in its day — weighing some 17 tons, 12 cwts, 1 qt, 15 lbs. When roads and bridges improved with the expansion of settlement, drivers upgraded from the steady bullocks to faster horses, which could cover some 20 to 30 kilometres a day. But they came at a price. Horses and their harnesses (including winkers, collars and hames, spiders, saddles and breeching for each of the shafters) cost decidedly more than yoked bullocks.

with rams from soil, climate and food source as much resembling his own as possible, and with a fleece of exactly the same character, besides being at least equal to his own stock in all points of quality. By the end of the 1850s Shaw was satisfied that the true Australian merino had been evolved in the Mt Emu Creek region (Western Victoria) and after a certain point was reached he became an advocate of colonial rams rather than imported sires. The debate over which was best rehearsed the birth pangs of Australian nationalism.

In 1859 Shaw was a founder of the influential Skipton Sheep Show, which ran until 1875 when it was overtaken by the Melbourne Sheep Show. A French judge presided. Similar events were to be increasingly held all over the country, marking a time when the Pure merinos came to town in their tweedy jackets and ties, their women in perky hats and fox furs, meeting their kind at Sydney's Australia Hotel or at the Melbourne, Adelaide, and Perth show-week equivalents. It was said that a win at Skipton was enough to raise any stud to prominence; the effect was multiplied at the later, larger shows. Prize rams were front page photo news; pretty girls nuzzled up to them; postage stamps bore their image; it was a Uardry (Riverina) ram struck on

the reverse side of the one shilling piece that symbolised Australian coinage until the image was culled by decimal currency in 1966 and replaced by a lyre bird (on the ten cent piece).

But this was looking way ahead. In 1851 the gold rushes pushed Australia on to the world stage economically and politically. Some of the loudest demands for parliamentary democracy came from the diggers of Ballarat and the Eureka stockade. Workers' voices would not be heard so pointedly or effectively (in fact much more effectively, finally) until the shearers' strikes of the 1890s, the repression and the imprisonments, and the election of labour governments that followed, to the amazement of the world. How could governments be owned by workers? They were the possession of capital. That is what they were for, weren't they?

How interesting that Australia would be one of the first countries in the world to question that assumption; and that when it came about it happened through sheep.

Victoria, now a separate colony from New South Wales, became the main centre of prosperity. Melbourne

The sun sets on another day of grazing. Sheep are actually very selective feeders. They prefer low-growing, fine plants and neglect the taller, more coarse species. In some parts of the country we are still paying the price for the overstocking that followed the first rush of European settlement. Debt-laden after a series of droughts, low prices and financial depressions in the 1800s, many sheep farmers placed enormous pressure on their soils and pastures by increasing stocking rates to disastrous levels.

would remain the financial capital of Australia until the late twentieth century, with nearby Geelong becoming Australia's veritable Fort Knox of the Golden Fleece. Between 1851 and 1860 Victoria's population increased seven times over while the country's total population tripled to more than one million, most of them unassisted immigrants of overwhelmingly British background. (A few Chinese entered the wool industry after this time; though widely despised for their racial origin they proved remarkable shearers and excellent shearing teachers, the legendary Jacky Howe learning from one.)

Now for the first time Australia had a consistent influx of educated, professionally and industrially skilled migrants. A good number of them would soon be making an impression on the wool industry — including FS Falkiner, Thomas Millear, Jonathon Shaw (son of Thomas Shaw), and the Peppins. The latter English family, their sheep breeding plans dominated by George Peppin junior, settled near Mansfield in Victoria, running cattle and sheep that were soon plagued by the main curses of the day, pleuropneumonia, footrot, scab and fluke — and so they took up land in the Riverina.

The fortunes of the Peppins symbolised what every expansionist pastoralist yearned for. They were in the right spot at the right time, yet it all seemed too hard, they hardly knew their luck and almost immediately tried selling out again. When they found no takers they seemed to blink, only then realising their advantages as they sketched out their ideal, a picture scrawled in the dust, the right sort of merino for their situation.

In its rough pioneering phase the Riverina had been principally cattle fattening country. Now was the moment when the swing back to sheep was happening in a big way, and just in time: cattle losses from pleuropneumonia would devastate the national herd with average annual losses at 125,000 head per year for the decade of the sixties.

The Peppin triumph was evoked in a key paragraph by Charles Massy in *The Australian Merino* (1990):

Working away in that fierce summer heat and dust, while developing backblock country and handling large numbers of stock from mid 1858 to mid 1861, those astute breeders would have noticed a number of things: that thin-locked, delicate fine wool broke down along the backs under the summer heat and let in dust; that small, weedy, dumpy animals could not cope with long distances and the environment; that the animals they desired for the meat market — quicker-fattening, robust

---

A memorial in Wanganella pays tribute to the Peppin family and the versatile merino they developed. The medium-woolled sheep was ideally suited to Australian conditions and has become our most productive strain.

types — were of a larger frame and longer leg; that the coarser-woolled sheep with broader backs and thicker wool withstood the fierce heat and dust better; and probably that a balance of nourishment in the wool — not too dry nor too greasy — was the best wool type to withstand dust and heat.

Having therefore observed and thought about what they had seen, the Peppins decided to let the environment have a major say in sheep type and to breed a sheep to suit the country. This was a major turning-point in the history of the merino.

Now the wool industry was getting more efficient, both financially and productively, it allowed for geographical expansion to take place unchecked. Australia's romantic frontier story celebrated in novels, poems, and ballads can be found in the push up through the western Riverina from the Victorian side, the taking of the lands of the Darling. It is there in Rolf Boldrewood's *Robbery Under Arms* and in a much later work, Joseph Furphy's *Such Is Life*. How drab to make it the subject of economic explanations — but how necessary if a full picture is to be suggested, truthful to the lives of those who work in paddocks with sheep.

In Europe and North America the wool textile industries were expanding and needed good raw product. By dint of experimentation with breeds and landscape Australia was ready with material. Enter in countless shiploads the shining Antipodean wools clipped in primitive dusty distances. A demand shift was underway, from clothing wools for the woollen industry towards combing wools for the worsted industry. Buying was concentrated through large spinners, merchant-combers and a few raw wool merchants, excluding middlemen wool merchants and encouraging economies of scale. Sale centres moved back to Australia and the whole place hummed, crackling to the bullocky's whip and the falsetto machine-rapid fire of the auctioneer. Between 1860 and 1900 the shift became complete and, overwhelmingly, the largest flocks grew combing wool. This was when for the first time it could be truly said that Australia coo-eed from the sheep's back.

Wool washing was phased out. No longer was anybody willing to pay a worthwhile premium for scoured wool. The swing towards greasy wool export became pronounced — cheaper freight rates after the spread of rail and riverboat transport meant extra weight in wool was not as crucial as when every inch of weary load strained the shoulders of bullocks, horse

The stylish Albury Railway Station opened in 1881 to facilitate the linking of Sydney and Melbourne by rail in 1883, which gave district woolgrowers a new transport option and hastened the demise of the romantic river transport. In due course rail would experience increasing competition from road transport.

teams, or in many places, especially in South Australia and the west, camel trains.

At the first cries of gold in the early 1850s, workers walked off stations everywhere. But by the end of the decade labour was in plentiful supply again, the workers were back on the station books, boiling down was a thing of the past, and the unique twang of fencing wire being unrolled was heard across the land — so much so that a negative side to fencing development eventually occurred, namely overstocking, or packing them in.

But after 1860 the dramatic effect of the introduction of wire fencing into sheep country could not be understated. It was prophetically and graphically advocated by TA Coghlan, New South Wales government statistician:

The country will carry one-third more sheep, the wool will be longer and sounder, and the fleece as a whole one-third better; the feed will be better and less liable to grass seed; the sheep will increase in size; they will live longer and continue longer profitable; they will be freer from footrot and other diseases; the expenses of working the station will be less than one quarter of what it would be if the sheep were shepherded; and finally, the owner will be able to devote the principal part of his time to improving his sheep instead of spending it in attempting to manage a number of shepherds and hut-keepers.

Fencing marched forward in step with sheep from this time on. The disasters and the try-outs of the nineteenth century shaped a shimmering image of the twentieth century to come.

Another factor in the revived demand for sheep was that because so much new country was being opened up, stocking and re-stocking demands were high. Anyone begetting them in numbers and turning out breeders in numbers was in a position to impress the banks. From 1860 onwards inventors were scratching their heads and developing mechanical shearing machines to handle the flood of sheep (machines took over after the late 1880s; their most persuasive feature being that they could remove more weight of wool, up to three quarters of a pound per animal). Darling River stations that had run cattle under difficulties became feasible for sheep with the introduction of river steamers as wool transporters. It was said that when the first paddle boat nosed up the Darling, station properties (let it not be thought they were grand affairs) doubled in value overnight.

These skilfully crafted wrought-iron gates lead to the church on Bungaree station, north of Clare, South Australia, which was built to service its large workforce of the 1800s.

Pastoral expansion now reached into the dry country outside the settled districts with their river and billabong frontages. It was a move made possible by technological change — well-sinking techniques, windmills, water troughs and again and again wire fencing materials. The artesian basin was tapped. Virtual sheep cathedrals, the big shearing sheds, were clad in corrugated iron, brilliantly stackable for transport by river, dray, and even by camel. Shearing sheds became icons of national architecture, their forms resonating in commercial and domestic structures far from the bush. When many people think of the industry, they think only of the sheds ennobling a fairly dirty and hard, unenviable job.

Settlement of inland Queensland proceeded apace within a wide swathe of country. From the south-west up to the Gulf there was another whole kingdom of land eventually proving suitable for sheep runs. In South Australia, where the word squatter was not appropriate, for the reason that land settlement had been more orderly and enlightened, graziers were on the way to creating a special breed of merino ready to be fed back into the east. To behold that colony's Bungaree wethers on the move was to see a long-legged animal more like an antelope than a sheep, or so it seemed to those who loved them and depended on them for their well-being in the red dust.

From the late nineteenth century where we leave the narrative of wool, the story moves through many more phases until it emerges again in Richard Woldendorp's photographic account.

Its present day character can still be seen in its origins, and vice versa. The story of wool is where many of our most unique expressions of culture are found — the voice of Australia, created out of dust and hot light. The language, the accent, the words barked at and over sheep. The birthplace of Australian nationalism and multiple aspects of the Australian character are located in the shearing sheds and the sheep paddocks of the far-flung states of the Commonwealth.

Wool Glossary

micron: the measure of wool's fibre diameter (one micron is one one-thousandth of a millimetre).

strong wool: wool comprising fibres of more than 22 microns in diameter.

medium wool: wool comprising fibres of 20.5 to 22 microns in diameter.

fine wool: wool comprising fibres of 18.6 to 20.5 microns in diameter.

superfine wool: wool comprising fibres of 18.5 microns and finer in diameter.

ultrafine: wool comprising fibres of 17.5 microns and finer in diameter.

heavy-cutting: sheep that produce a lot of wool.

long-stapled: wool with long staples, the natural clusters of wool fibres.

1

THE LAND

Australia has the largest sheep industry in the world and sheep can be found today in almost every corner except the wet tropics and the Northern Territory. Merinos, especially, have proved versatile and hardy, thriving on a variety of natural and improved pastures from the parched Murchison in Western Australia to the emerald valleys of Tasmania.

Shrouded in mist, the rich grazing flats of Severn Park (above) are dwarfed by the main range of the Snowy Mountains near Cooma. Cold and dry, the basalt and granite country of the Monaro was first taken up in the 1820s and 1830s and it soon established itself as a prime breeding ground, producing adaptable sheep that perform well just about anywhere in Australia. Major studs like Hazeldean and Middle View continue that proud tradition today, producing fine to medium-woolled sheep with high yielding fleeces thanks, in part, to the region's good ground cover and minimal dust.

Sheep tracks etch the burnished summer plains surrounding a watering point near Northam, east of Perth (opposite). Sheep are remarkably hardy animals and, in Australia, have adapted to a variety of conditions. But drought — as inevitable as flies — has routinely culled the nation's flock. In the mid nineteenth century desperate graziers were forced to boil down thousands of sheep for tallow to recoup losses. About 19 million sheep died throughout the country during the 1901–03 drought, reducing our sheep numbers from 72 to 53 million. Sheep forced to walk long distances across dusty paddocks to reach water not only exacerbate food shortages around dwindling water supplies but produce lower yielding fleeces.

From the saltbush country of the Nullarbor between Eucla and Cocklebiddy (above) to the sparse Murchison district in Western Australia (left) the Australian landscape has accommodated sheep in vast numbers. Early breeders soon realised that Australia's coarse herbage, dust and climatic extremes demanded a big, robust sheep that grew strong, heavy, long-stapled wool. So began the lengthy and complex process of breeding sheep, as Charles Massy describes in *The Australian Merino*, 'calculated for the country.' The merino strains that evolved proved highly suitable, thriving on spinifex, saltbush or grasslands, their fleeces protected by a high natural grease content. However the climate, soil and vegetation types within each wool-growing region in Australia continue to influence the quality of wool produced.

A mauve sunset envelopes another day south of Albury, in southern New South Wales. On the border of the Riverina and Monaro sheep zones, this region produces everything from superfine to broad wools but overall production has declined dramatically in recent years. The volatility of wool prices and threat of Johne's disease has seen many traditional woolgrowers opt instead for dryland cropping (largely canola and maize) and lamb fattening.

Tasmania boasts some of Australia's finest sheep — and most picturesque rural scenery. This mob graze in the north, near Devonport, but it is the central and northern Midlands that produce some of Australia's best superfine wool-clips. Home to the Saxon-type merino strain developed by Eliza Forlonge and others, the region known as the Macquarie Valley was long regarded the merino stud farm of Australia. From the 1850s to the 1870s Midlands stock had a profound influence on the genetics of the Australian sheep flock but as the mainland's pastoral zones developed, the Saxon breeds could not compete with the more versatile Peppin strains. Although the dual-purpose Polwarth and Corriedale breeds rose to prominence in Tasmania in the early 1900s merinos again dominate today, comprising some 75 per cent of the total flock.

A misty morning dawns in northern Tasmania. Clean pastures, relatively free of dust and burrs, help produce some 10 per cent of the nation's superfine fleeces just south of here, in the compact and exclusive Midlands wool-growing district. Sheep are grazed on improved pastures in the Macquarie River valleys and native pastures in the surrounding dolerite hills in what can best be described as cool-temperate, dry climatic conditions.

In the rush for land early squatters sometimes gave little thought to location and convenience when establishing their runs, but a reliable water source was always cherished, whether it be Billabong Creek in the Riverina (opposite) or Stockade Creek in central Queensland (above).

Remote pastoralists relied on determined bullockies and later river transport and railway links to ease their isolation. Over time, as land productivity has been improved, Australian sheep properties have shrunk in size but the physical environment remains an important determinant of wool quality. Breeding improvements are as much a product of soil, pasture and other environmental factors as they are of genetics, and water remains a precious resource.

Japanese and Italian wool buyers have helped foster the development of superfine wools in Tasmania in recent times, paying top dollar for fleeces produced in the Midlands, where the serpentine Macquarie River slithers through a patchwork of paddocks in the Longford area. Some 75 per cent of the state's superfine wool is bought by Italian manufacturers, with Korea emerging as a buyer of secondary stature. The strong, bright, soft-handling wools are favoured for their reliability in processing.

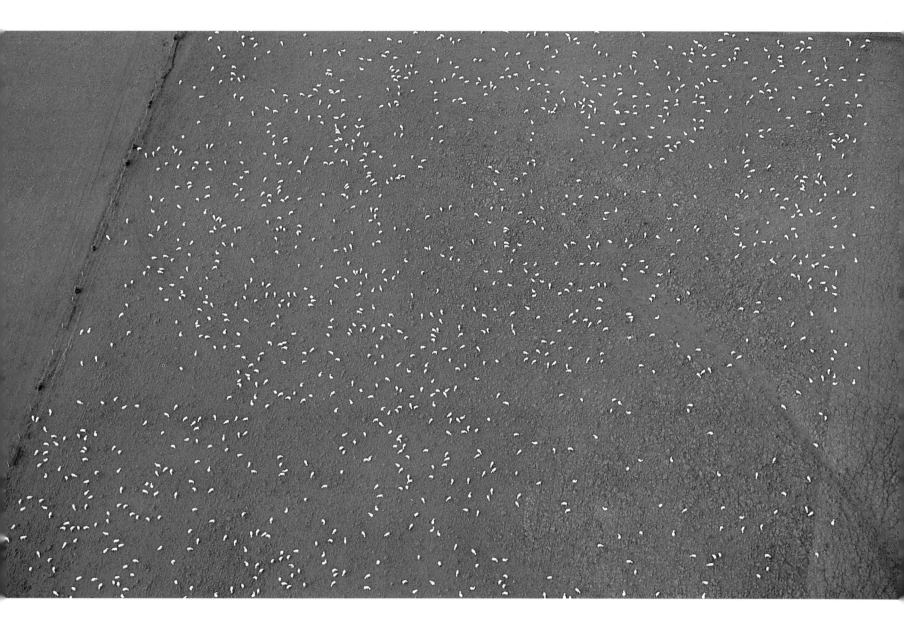

Like maggots crawling on the skin of the earth, sheep dot a paddock near Longford, in Tasmania. Tasmania's flock is small by mainland standards — just four million — but its sheep are hardy, surviving in sometimes tough conditions. A cleft upper lip enables a sheep to graze close to the ground but it must feed for many hours a day to extract the nutrients it needs. The average economic life of a sheep is eight years, comprising 6-8 shearings.

Valuable Collinsville Stud rams (above) graze contentedly in the shadow of the North Mount Lofty Ranges, just north of Hallett. One of the most influential studs in Australia, Collinsville was established in 1895 and specialises in breeding prepotent stud sires. Buyers clamour for its rams, particularly in South Australia, where the stud has repeatedly broken the world auction price record for merino rams. The large-framed sheep can withstand all elements while achieving high lambing percentages and producing heavy-cutting fleeces of 22–24 microns. Each year the stud joins (mates) just under 10,000 stud ewes, sells more than 3500 rams and produces 1500 bales of wool. Its rams have sold to the world's major wool-producing countries, including Argentina, Uruguay, Mexico, New Zealand, the former USSR, China, South Africa and the United States and its stock are said to influence more than one-third of the Australian wool-clip today.

Rolling out to the horizon as flat and as far as the eye can see, the great Riverina plains (left) promised and delivered much to the early pastoralists. The central and western Riverina is home to some of our most notable sheep studs, including Wanganella — the cradle of the Peppin merino strain that is now the most numerous and productive wool-growing sheep in the world. Nearly three-quarters of Australian sheep today are descended from the famous merinos developed by George Peppin junior and his brothers and some 26 parent studs now dapple the riverine plains, which are ideally suited to the production of medium merino wool. Low rainfall — as little as 330 millimetres a year — is supplemented by irrigation. Inspiration for Burrinjuck Dam (1926), serving the Murrumbidgee Irrigation Area, came from engineering works conducted by pastoralist Sir Samuel McCaughey on Coonong and North Yanco around the turn of the century.

South Australia's vast grazing potential, typified by this rich pastoral land south of Burra (above) enticed settlers in the late 1830s and early 1840s. The exhaustion of available land in Victoria and drought in New South Wales saw great mobs of sheep overlanded into South Australia and by the end of 1840 its sheep population totalled some 200,160. In the years that followed, South Australian breeders working in geographic and genetic isolation developed new and superior strong-wool merino strains, suited to the drier parts of the state, that were to have a profound impact on Australian sheep breeds. These sheep could survive on what little herbage was available and their strong wools could withstand dust penetration and the damaging effect of the sun's rays. Across the then loosely defined border in western Victoria, sheep farmers in the mid-1800s battled outbreaks of virulent scab, as attested by this place name

(below) near Edenhope. A series of Scab Acts in force from 1832 to 1870 sought to contain the spread of the disease by prohibiting the movement of infected sheep and threatening hefty fines but it still spread like wildfire. An official report in 1865 stated 'the magnitude of this evil is such that it must intimately affect the well-being of the whole community' and by 1867 New South Wales had imposed a total ban on Victorian sheep crossing the border. Afflicted animals were often treated with a cocktail of water, tobacco and corrosive chemicals that sound far worse than the disease itself. But the diligence paid off and scab was eradicated from Victoria by 1877.

Interlopers themselves, sheep have encountered a variety of threats, both natural and feral, in the Australian landscape. Rabbits, dogs, kangaroos and to a lesser extent wild pigs have all taken their toll and remain the sheep's greatest rivals, especially during periods of drought.

Rabbits that hopped ashore in 1859 bred and spread rapidly and remained largely unchecked until the introduction of the myxoma virus in 1951 and more recent releases of the calicivirus. Native dingoes and feral dogs continue to ravage flocks periodically, particularly in central and southern Queensland and along the Great Dividing Range, prompting intermittent baiting and trapping campaigns. And then there are the far-ranging locals — kangaroos.

In extending grasslands, deterring dingoes, removing Aborigines and providing permanent water supplies for their stock, graziers have inadvertently encouraged some species of kangaroo. Although several recent studies have concluded that sheep do not compete with kangaroos for some herbage, leaving certain grasses for kangaroos to dine on exclusively, some kangaroo species have undoubtedly benefited from pasture improvements. Others, namely the smaller kangaroos, have been forever lost due to stock grazing pressures and extensive land clearing. It's the roos' appetite for scarce herbage and water during droughts that raises the ire of sheep graziers most: sheep are thought to require four times as much water as their bounding neighbours.

Dingo trapper Kevin Campbell (above) sets some traps in the hope of snaring wild dogs near Blackall. The former Blackall Shire dogger and now freelance operator has trapped 800 wild dogs, almost all of them dingoes, over the past five years, practising an art that is fast disappearing. It's a time-consuming, secretive and lonely job; Kevin routinely spends weeks camping in the bush trying to discover where the dogs live and drink before setting traps. He says the move from sheep into cattle in his district has given cockies a false sense of security. 'They think that if they go into cattle the dingoes won't worry them but they can do just as much damage to cattle and horses,' he says. 'A lot of the old dog-netting fences aren't maintained anymore either.'

Blackall professional shooter Ron Morgan (below) sets his sights on a kangaroo to add to his overnight tally. Ron shoots between 10 and 100 roos each evening, depending on the weather conditions, and has watched numbers in central Queensland steadily grow during his

20 year career. 'Conditions are better for roos today, with abundant water and feed, but property owners hate them because they eat all the grasses and destroy fences,' he says. A local pet-food company processes about 800 kangaroos a day but Ron sends the wild boars he shoots — sometimes 10-15 a night — to Longreach for processing and subsequent sale to Germany. 'Farmers also like us to rid their places of pigs because they take a fair few lambs during the lambing season,' he says.

As in many other parts of Australia, the woolgrowers of the Murchison district in Western Australia have historically relied upon natural water supplies like this billabong. When rivers dry up such vestiges keep stock alive and dreams afloat.

The blue expanse of Wooleen Lake laps at the heart of Wooleen station (above) just one year in seven on average. Covering some 190,000 hectares in the Murchison district, 700 kilometres north-east of Perth, Wooleen is at the northernmost limit of the voluminous sheep and cattle country in Western Australia and owners Brett and Helen Pollock rely largely on natural mulga rangelands, saltbush and winter wildflowers to support their 14,000 sheep. 'We run to a minimum, which gives us a buffer when times get tough,' says Brett. 'This also helps conserve our rangelands.' The major challenges of running a property this size, according to Brett, are maintaining the 852 kilometres of fencing and 52 windmills, preventing overgrazing and keeping sheep well hydrated during the 50-degree summer days.

The wide brown land of poet Dorothea Mackellar's verse is evoked in this aerial view (opposite) of Yeadon station, north-east of Hay. Here the Rutledge family have bred sheep for three generations, enduring unseasonally dry conditions over the past decade. 'All you can do is feed them, lighten off the stocking and battle on,' says Michael Rutledge. 'It's all about perseverance.' Numbers have come back by 30 per cent to 30,000 medium merinos in recent times and the family has occasionally had to resort to costly supplementary feeding with oats, lucerne and corn. Although merinos, with bloodlines running back to Spain and North Africa, Saxony, Silesia, and France, weren't built for Australian conditions, it can sometimes seem as if they were, and stronger-wool types have flourished on the drier western plains of New South Wales on a primary diet of saltbush.

Soil erosion (opposite) savagely scars the landscape east of Northam, in Western Australia. Australia's ride to prosperity on the sheep's back has come at a high price and farmers are only now coming to grips with wide-scale erosion caused by decades of overgrazing and land clearing. The process of environmental degradation began in the late 1800s, with massive overstocking of sheep and cattle, severe droughts, financial depressions and rabbit plagues. Throughout much of Australia the protective layer of plants and shrubs was stripped away, exposing our heavily weathered soils. Then the climate — long, dry, windy spells broken by heavy downpours — has caused erosion and cloven-hoofed animals like sheep (considered 'four-legged vacuum cleaners' by environmentalist Vincent Serventy) have further compacted the soil and restricted plant growth. These days, sheep farmers recognise that the soil feeds the sheep and we have entered an era of land restoration and soil conservation. The profusion of Paterson's curse, or Salvation Jane, in a paddock near Northam (above) is a sign of severe pasture depletion although sheep can feed on its green foliage. The abundance of poisonous plants was another hazard to Western Australian sheep-farmers, who unwittingly suffered widespread sheep losses during the early days of settlement.

Australia's first sheep graziers sometimes defined their holdings with a mere furrow and relied on watchful but company-starved shepherds to protect and contain their flocks. They tolerated the tedious sorting of stray sheep, periodic thefts, trespassing and stock ownership disputes until land tenure became more permanent, stock routes had been exhausted and the vast sheep runs were broken up by closer settlement.

Fencing represented a substantial capital expense and most squatters could only afford it after the profitable times of the 1850s and 1860s. The first boundary fences were built of brush, chock and log, then post-and-rail or stones. But fencing was not adopted on a large scale until the introduction of fencing wire, which fortuitously became available just as the shepherds were abandoning their flocks to try their luck in the goldfields.

Fencing wire entered Victoria in the early 1850s; it was relatively cheap, and fences could be erected quickly and easily repaired. A writer in the 1860s described how a run of 311 square kilometres that had employed 13 shepherds and seven hut-keepers could be managed by six boundary riders after it had been fenced into paddocks. By 1870 there were more than 32,000 kilometres of fencing in New South Wales alone and by 1880 this had strung out to more than 300,000 kilometres.

As well as saving pastoralists considerable labour costs fences helped to improve stock health and sheep management. Sheep were healthier when they grazed freely in paddocks, lambing percentages increased, fewer lambs died and the wool was cleaner. This all meant that paddocks could be stocked with more sheep, potentially increasing earnings. It was a little later before fencing was also recognised as a practical means of genetic management — of ensuring controlled joinings and isolating valuable imported or improved bloodstock.

Road workers do some running repairs on a stock grid north of Goodooga, in far northern New South Wales. Although grids have done away with gates in some station country and are an effective means of property separation, they still require regular maintenance.

Rusted but ever reliable, a disused section of the barrier fence near the Nullarbor Roadhouse spans part of the Nullarbor Plain, where it has headed off rabbits and dingoes for almost a century. Some private landholders had erected individual fences and employed doggers before the single, continuous fence was completed to protect sheep country to the south. It is still effective against wild dogs today, provided it remains secure, and routine inspections are carried out to repair damage. The rapid and relentless rabbit incursions that helped inspire the fence's construction are now but a memory but it reputedly cost Otway Falkiner £120,000 in 1894 to combat the plague on his Riverina property Boonoke. One of his sons later recalled: 'One of the worst jobs I had to do was clean out the rabbit bays along the fences. Dead and stinking rabbits were waist-high around me as I worked.'

Wool-grower Brian Fraser has gone to electric lengths to bar wild dogs from his Tallangatta property in northern Victoria. His 100-kilometre, 1.2-metre fence strung with four electric and four earth wires, cost more than $100,000 and countless hours to construct but has been effective in excluding wild dogs residing in the surrounding state forest. 'I have lost thousands of sheep, about 700 lambs in one year alone some twenty years back, so while it's been very labour-intensive and capital costly and requires constant maintenance, I'm successfully protecting my sheep,' says Brian. Although a 5412 kilometres dingo fence continues to protect parts of pastoral Queensland, New South Wales and South Australia some pastoralists are erecting electric fences of their own in wild dog 'blackspots' like northern Victoria and south-eastern South Australia.

A stone fence snakes off into the grass near Colac in southern Victoria. Such fences, built throughout Australia, served the dual purpose of containing stock while also helping clear paddock of rocks. They were especially common from the 1850s to the 1870s in western Victoria, where an abundance of volcanic rock provided ready building materials for tradesman from Scotland, Ireland, Wales and England. Some of the stone fences were dismantled and re-erected in the period from 1868 to 1870 to ensure they were rabbit-proof but a surprising number survive intact today, mostly on the older pastoral properties around Camperdown. Pastoralists were soon won over to the practice of running sheep in fenced paddocks without shepherds after witnessing improvements in sheep health.

Looking west from the hills east of Campbell Town, over typical sheep grazing country, central Tasmania.

2

MUSTERING

The romantic idyll of the outback mustering team on horseback, draped in billowing dust amid a swirling mob of sheep, has been largely relegated to the annals of history. Since the advent of motorised transport pastoralists have increasingly employed a combination of motorbikes, helicopters and even light planes and gyrocopters to bring sheep in to the yards. But some old habits die hard. Ears pricked and eyes intent, the working dog remains an indispensable member of the mustering team.

Up until the early 1980s horses were the most common mode of mustering transport on Nangetty station (above), west of Geraldton, in Western Australia. In those days the station employed six jackeroos, an overseer and head stockman, several house helpers and 12 shearers at shearing time. Back in the 1920s some 20 experienced Aboriginal stockmen were on the payroll. These days the 10,000 medium-woolled merinos are mustered using motorbikes and a single vehicle, and staffing has been dramatically reduced. 'Some still see the pastoralist as king but the golden age is over,' says family matriarch Nan Broad.

In a marriage of old and new, Curbur station staff used a helicopter, dogs and motorbike (opposite) in the 1980s to bring sheep in to their Murchison sheds. More recently Keros and Simone Keynes have hired a piloted light aircraft and paid motorbike mustering contractors to share the job. Their 10,000 sheep are commonly pushed through laneways or collected in holding paddocks scattered around the 202,500 hectare property, from where they are retrieved for shearing. 'The pilot communicates with the guys on the bikes, who have their own vehicles and dogs,' says Simone. 'Aerial support is a must in this scrubby breakaway country.'

Chopper power. Helicopters (above) have given woolgrowers operating vast inland properties a new perspective on managing their land and stock, and are a very welcome mustering aid. Although expensive to run or hire, choppers are efficient and highly manoeuvrable for aerial reconnaissance and are equally effective in handling sheep when used in conjunction with ground-based teams on motorbikes with dogs. Especially where distances are great and properties are scrubby, choppers save thousands of kilometres on farm bikes and reduce the number of ground staff needed. 'Using horses with dogs is too labour-intensive and impractical in this area of the western division,' says Graham Brown of Reola station, who uses two helicopters and a gyrocopter to muster and handle stock throughout the year.

Stockmen rev up and rug up against the cold morning (opposite) as another day of droving begins on Rawlinna station in south-eastern Western Australia. Plucking sheep out of the mulga and myall scrub and driving them across the bluebush plains starts one month out from shearing, using eight motorbikes, and the sheep converge from as far as 100 kilometres distant. At 3.5 million acres (roughly the size of Israel), Rawlinna is one of the largest sheep stations in Australia, employing 12 staff to care for some 75,000 sheep. 'It takes one and a half hours to drive from the homestead to the outstation and to drive from one end of the property to the other takes four hours,' says manager Ross Wood. 'It's hot in summer and we get the cold winds off the Bight in winter but you just have to have confidence and hang in there.'

Ever alert and willing, good working dogs are an asset to a sheep property and kelpies (above) form the backbone of Australia's four-legged mustering work force. Top breeders say a paddock dog ideally must show anticipation, good natural distance from stock, natural heading ability, and a light to moderate amount of eye — qualities determined by their genetics. 'Eye' is the stare the dog uses to control the sheep, it gives the sheep the impression they are being stalked. A dog must also have a good capacity to learn. 'A good working kelpie is one of the most intelligent dogs in the world,' boasts breeder Nancy Withers. While motorbikes have revolutionised sheep work, largely replacing horses, they have not caused farmers to dispense with dogs. In fact, many dogs now travel to their place of work in style, much faster. Mustering dogs are especially valued in areas where the terrain is inaccessible to motorbikes, including the highlands of New South Wales and the Flinders Ranges. For Russell Poole at Malboona station in Queensland (opposite) and Haddon Rig, in western New South Wales (right), man and dog form a balanced partnership.

Calling all drovers. School holiday recruits on Muloorina station in central South Australia (above), take a less orthodox approach to mustering, co-ordinating their efforts on horseback, motorbike and in a battered buggy. The station, covering 4000 square kilometres (one million acres) south-east of Lake Eyre (opposite), is run by brothers Malcolm and Trevor Mitchell and their families, and no-one is idle when it comes time to shear the 5000 strong-woolled sheep. Over 10 days the junior mustering team feed the 16-strong shearers with mobs gathered from the surrounding sandhills and gibber plains. 'Back in the 1970s we used to shear 30,000 sheep and it would take us seven weeks,' says Malcolm. 'Through the 1990s wool wasn't worth anything and we went for seven years without making any money so we scaled right back and went into cattle, but the sheep are coming good now.'

Fast, intelligent and willing (how is it that they seem to enjoy their job so much?), the sheepdog is a priceless asset — a sheep-farmer's faithful work-mate and loyal friend. It's difficult to estimate the number of working dogs in service in Australia. Even the smaller sheep farms usually have one or two and some of the larger stations in more inhospitable country boast an entire tail-wagging pack. The kelpie and border collie — our two main sheepdog breeds — are distinctive and valued for their different attributes but both breeds originated from collies imported to Australia from Scotland before 1870. The dogs bred more recently to tolerate our harsh conditions continue to command respect and admiration, here and abroad.

The sheep penned, now it's time for a dip at the Avenpart Kelpie Stud (right), near Wanganella in New South Wales. The kelpie is a lean and strong breed capable of withstanding the extremes of Australian temperatures. The dogs are respected for their stamina, courage and desire to work, but their active lifestyle, lived close to the ground, puts them at risk of heat exhaustion. Depending on its natural ability and training, a good dog is said to be capable of doing the work of up to seven people but even the smartest individual has not yet mastered the art of opening a gate (below).

Top dog (opposite). Unlike paddock dogs, which are largely silent and must maintain a distance from sheep, specialist yard and shed dogs use their bark and physical contact to achieve results. Sheep possess acute hearing and have excellent stereoscopic vision. In a paddock they can see a dog over 500 metres away and can even see backwards through their rear legs while grazing. The dog exacts control by relying on a sheep's instinctive fear.

The kelpie breed is lauded for its speed and agility. All stud kelpies are registered with the Working Kelpie Council and a well-bred registered dog can fetch as much as $4000 to 7000 — a small price to pay, say breeders, for sometimes a decade of determined and devoted service. Sheepdogs can be taught to respond to hand, whistle or voice signals and most reputable studs give a replacement guarantee with pups and dogs sold for a specific purpose.

Stylish temporary digs await this mob (right) on the southern Victorian farm run by Charles and Patricia Laidlawe. The L-shaped bluestone shearing shed, built in 1886, is one of several in the western district made using this distinctive local material.

The sun sets on another successful muster (opposite).

3

SHEARING SHEDS

Entering an old lanolin-smeared shearing shed, the air redolent with sweat and sheep shit and stories, evokes an indelible sense of history. In his book *Shearing Life in Australia,* Ray Sherman describes woolsheds as 'the closest thing to an old jumper that one can think of.' And woolsheds come in a variety of shapes and sizes, some bulging at the seams and others worn thin and holey.

Important though the shearing shed is, it is only in use for a few weeks of the year so most designs have remained relatively simple. Beginning with structures little more than bough shelters, the Australian sheds grew with the size of the flocks and the wool cheques, but largesse was never a guarantee of comfort. Functionality was paramount and poor ventilation and bad lighting the norm. Many were designed according to local custom that invariably put the needs of the sheep above those who worked them.

Minor architectural refinements have accompanied improved shearing practices but little has changed on the factory floor in decades. That so many original sheds have survived is a testament to the quality of the original craftsmanship, the sturdiness of the building materials and the commitment of maintenance-minded property owners with a healthy respect for history.

Sunlight seeps through the weathered timbers of the former Gol Gol station shearing shed (opposite), now contained within Mungo National Park, in the Lachlan–Darling backblocks of south-western New South Wales. Settled in 1868 by the Peppins of Wanganella fame, Gol Gol didn't boast magnificent sheep feed but was just 35 miles (55 km) from Pooncarie — a central shipping point for wool and supplies on the Darling River. The 45-metre-long shed was built in 1869 by Chinese labourers using termite-resistant, pit-sawn Murray pine for the framework, mallee sticks for gates and corrugated iron for the roofing (above). Lined up along the 30 stands shearers defleeced 50,000 sheep each year. Gol Gol remained a pastoral property until sold to the New South Wales government in 1978.

Glimmering from a new paint job, the Deeargee shearing shed (above) 12 kilometres east of Uralla wears its age well. Deeargee and nearby Gostwyck stations formed part of the substantial holdings of noted New England pastoralist William Dangar until the properties were split in 1969. The first construction phase of the shed included the unusual octagonal shearing board (opposite) built in 1872 that could accommodate 80 blade shearers. Further enlargements — a central section to house mechanical shearing machines (22 stands) and a brick extension for new classing bins, wool press and wool bale storage — were made in 1889 and 1903 respectively. Today some 24,000 fine and superfine merinos pass through the National Trust-listed shed during the July–August shearing. 'It's an important building in the region's heritage and some aspects of the design are innovative even today,' says co-owner Hugh Sutherland. 'Many people admiring the octagonal section ask if it's the upstairs shearing quarters.'

An eerie stillness descends on the Tubbo shearing shed (above) but come late April it's hard to hear yourself think amid the din of the overhead gear and the hum of the hydraulic press. In the late 1880s 100 shearers bent their backs to shear between 50,000 and 80,000 woollies on what was then the largest freehold property in Australia. The darkened holding pens, starved of light to keep the sheep calm, were crafted from cedar, imported Oregon and cypress pine milled on the Riverina property. The boiler from the old steam plant that once powered the mechanical shears is still fired up — these days to guarantee a hot shower at day's end for the 16-strong shearing team.

Ingenious casement gates distinguish the holding pens within Werocata station's shearing shed (opposite), now ghostly quiet north-west of Balaklava in South Australia. Not a single sheep grazes the station these days — the Oldfield family run 1000 head of cattle instead — but the shed survives as testimony to the heady days when 100,000 crossed the board.

Prefabricated steel was shipped 12,500 nautical miles from England to Brisbane, then railed 1000 kilometres to Ilfracombe and carted 128 kilometres by bullock dray to construct the distinctive half-moon shearing shed in central Queensland in 1914. It was a stylish, if costly, replacement for the original shed, burnt down by arsonists in 1912. The brainchild of progressive owners Sir Rupert Clarke and Robert Whiting, the steel and iron-skinned building was all electric and pioneered a circular board now prized by woolgrowers and an early model hydraulic press. Today the 234,000 hectare property is owned by Kerry Packer and 50,000 medium-wool sheep now graze its open Mitchell grass plains, broken boree and gidgee country.

A misty veil on Meadowbank Lake lifts to reveal the Lawrenny shearing shed, managed and used by a collective of Tasmanian woolgrowers since the conclusion of World War Two. The shed was developed by the Agricultural Development Bank as part of a soldier settlement scheme to cater for 40,000 to 50,000 sheep grazed in the immediate surrounds. Growers continue to pay an annual levy per head of sheep shorn and are jointly responsible for maintenance but shed use has declined and just 20,000 are now shorn there each year. 'It was vital in the formative years and it still represents a considerable capital saving but a number of factors have conspired against a group shearing shed,' says trust member Chris Johnston, who continues to use it. 'There's concern about the risk of footrot and lice infection and the distances sheep have to be moved. We shear in winter now and need to get the pregnant ewes back to their paddocks quickly, so many growers have opted to build their own sheds.'

The cypress pine and Oregon innards of expansive Toganmain shearing shed are scratched with the initials of shearers who have shorn there for over a century. It originally accommodated 100 blade shearers and was one of the first stations in the Riverina to use shearing machines (75 stands). The Wolseley Sheep Shearing Machine Company demonstrated their machine here in 1887 and 15 were installed in 1888 — the same year that Dunlop station, on the Darling River near Louth, became the first shed to use machines for its entire shearing. Toganmain recalls the grandeur of the old days when shearing was concentrated in a few large sheds and upwards of 200 men sweated their way through sometimes 200,000 sheep at a time. Now part of Gundaline — one of the biggest freehold properties in New South Wales, owned by the Twynam Pastoral Company — the shed still sees 32,000 sheep at shearing but is showing its age. 'The shed was built for another era, when sheep were half the size and you didn't have occupational health and safety issues to be concerned about,' says Gundaline livestock manager Nick Wragge. 'But the craftsmanship, the smell and the atmosphere of the shed is amazing. Tens of millions of sheep would have passed through it and the building has held up remarkably well.'

By the end of the nineteenth century the large sheds were clamouring for machines and 72 were installed at Tuppal woolshed (above and opposite) in 1900. Two years later 207,515 sheep were recorded as being shorn in this cavernous building, fashioned largely from Murray pine and corrugated iron. Some of the original brick-paved yards and several gracious sugar gums also survive from the era when shearers stretched for almost 90 metres along the board. The first sheds typically allowed for one shearing stand per 1000 sheep. So big was one shed — at Big Burrawong — that a brothel reportedly operated successfully alongside. Often solitary, with ample room for holding yards, the shed was best sited in a central location. Sheds today are much more modest and more likely to accommodate 4 to 12 stands.

Prince among the South Australian sheds is Anlaby —
an impressive stone monument to the heady days of
sheep farming in the nineteenth century. Founded in
1839, the historic station is the state's oldest extant
merino stud and its grand woolshed (above), north of
Kapunda, recalls the days when 50,000 sheep kept
36 blade shearers in steady employment for weeks on
end. The reddish sandstone was quarried locally and
Oregon imported for the frame and internal joinery
(left). About 1500 sheep — enough for 2 to 3 days of
shearing — can be housed inside the spacious shed,
which is now listed with the National Trust.

There's no shortage of cover for sheep being shorn at Dunumbral shed, with provision for 800 woollies in the shed itself, 400 beneath the board and a further 400 in a nearby shed. Shearers refuse to shear wet sheep, contesting that they pose a health risk, producing rheumatism or even more serious ailments. Of perhaps greater concern to the woolgrower is the threat of fire in bales of wet wool caused by spontaneous combustion. Wool absorbs moisture readily from the atmosphere and wet wool can deteriorate rapidly. Sheep kept cool are also considered easier to shear; when hot they tend to be overactive. They must also be shorn on an empty stomach; a bellyful makes shearing uncomfortable for sheep and shearer alike.

A small valley secretes the main farm and residential buildings of Dennistoun station (above), 8 kilometres north of Bothwell in central Tasmania, but it is the surrounding stony hills that sustain its 15,000 medium merinos. The 4050 hectare property has been in the Edgell family since 1913 — just six years after the weatherboard shearing shed (left) was built. At 14 stands it was once one of the largest in the island state. Today, just six stands are used at shearing and the Edgells have diversified their farming operation — growing opium poppies, peas and lupins, thanks to Clyde River irrigation, as well as running Angus cattle that are part of the oldest Angus herd in Australia. Stock numbers declined dramatically in southern Tasmania during the droughts of the 1990s and sheep numbers are only now beginning to build again. 'This is a dry part of Tasmania, with rather uncertain seasons and sometimes heavy frosts and we often have a winter deficit of feed but otherwise it's pretty kind to us,' says Henry Edgell.

The honeycomb rock used in 1852 to construct the woolshed (opposite) at Mount Hesse station, near Winchelsea in southern Victoria, was somewhat softer than the bluestone found elsewhere in the state and could be worked by less skilled craftsmen. The property has been in the family of David Kininmonth since 1882 and, like his forebears, he continues to shepherd fine sheep — these days some 18,500, including fat lambs. The property was named after explorer Hesse, who with Gellibrand explored and opened up this area near Mortlake in Victoria.

BUILDING MATERIALS

A variety of materials, both local and imported, have been used in the construction of Australia's functional woolsheds. The first buildings were mostly of post and beam construction, using heavy logs, plain or adzed, that were jointed and locked together using timber pegs or hand-made nails. Balloon framing followed, in which precision-cut rectangular sectional timbers were butt-joined and fixed together with factory-made nails. Corrugated iron replaced shingle roofs from the mid-1800s onwards and machine-sawn weatherboards were a welcome development for cladding walls.

In western Victoria basalt rock called bluestone was commonly used in shed construction; elsewhere limestone and pink dolomite were favoured, and when bricks were used they were usually quarried on site and sometimes laid by indentured labourers.

Stories and sweat are sealed within the doors (top left) and walls (top right) of station buildings throughout Australia.

The grey skeletal counting-out pens at Mogila station (bottom left) in northern New South Wales, testify to the durability of gidgee. This timber is used throughout the shearing shed, built in 1913.

Afternoon light warms the battened floor (bottom right) of this typical woolshed. The slats aid air circulation and allow sheep droppings to pass through to the ground below. Cleanliness in a shed is important to prevent infection, blood poisoning and tetanus in sheep. Elevating a shed also stopped timber rot and provided room below to keep additional sheep dry — just as important today as it was more than one hundred and fifty years ago.

The sun and an era sets on a shed near Carcoar, in the New South Wales Central West (opposite). Much early merino breeding was conducted in this district but many sheds, this one among them, have fallen into disrepair, abandoned in the shift from sheep to cattle over the past ten to fifteen years. Droughts and overgrazing, rabbits, dingoes, the sheep blowfly, labour shortages and global economics have all contributed to sheep being withdrawn from some of their original runs. The more stubborn wool producers have had to adopt better land management and water conservation strategies, judiciously control diseases and improve pastures to remain viable. Where they have been successful stocking rates have increased and fleeces have grown heavier — rising from an average of 2.7 kilograms in 1880 to 4.5 kilograms in 1989.

Severn Park (above) — an elegant study in corrugated iron. Most of the architecture within the shearing complex of this Monaro property features this evocative building material. In the early days of Australian settlement, it was cheap, light and versatile and therefore readily accepted across the range of Australian climates. Many a cargo ship transporting wool to Britain returned with this rippled iron as ballast in its belly. It was ideal for roofing, replacing the shingles and bark roofs of old; it could be used to clad walls, and was ideal for making tanks, gutters and downpipes.

Limestone was the fashion in South Australia for shearing sheds and quarters like this (opposite, top) north of Tintinara, in the south-east, thanks to the underlying karst system. An old blade shed, it was never converted to machine shearing. Soil deficiencies identified in 1936 that made the wool brittle put an end to wool-growing. The addition of trace elements has since restored the soil quality somewhat, but sheep are no longer run and the enduring shed is used only on social occasions.

A number of stone shearing sheds like this one at Morambro (opposite, bottom) punctuate the limestone country around Naracoorte, in South Australia. Architect William Thomas Gore was responsible for several of the T-shaped shed designs in the district and a recent historical study by Adelaide architect Andrew Klenke revealed that these substantial stone woolsheds appeared early in South Australia — the 1850s and 1860s — making them possibly the first examples of major property improvements in the country. 'I was surprised at the care taken and attention to detail; they were probably better built than they needed to be,' says Andrew. 'I see them as status symbols of that early sheep success.' Some of the buildings were thought to have been constructed by Chinese labourers indentured to landholders. 'It's a basic structure but very spacious and it can hold a lot of sheep,' says Morambro owner Tim Donaldson. 'It wasn't built to suit today's shearing practices but it was certainly built to last.'

Rough-hewn boree timbers, worn somewhat smoother by lanolin lubrication, form the bones of the Thornleigh station shed, west of Blackall. The shed was there when Buddie Wagstaff's grandfather John Henry bought the station in 1912 and unlike others in the district it has changed little since, with the exception of a new hardwood floor. 'Many people moving from sheep into cattle have pulled the guts out of their shearing sheds and turned them into machinery sheds,' says Buddie, who continues to delight in seeing 12,000 sheep go through the Thornleigh shed each July.

A dose of drench post-shearing and this mob will soon be returned to the sprawling paddocks of Rawlinna station, in Western Australia. Sheds like this at the Rawlinna outcamp were designed to facilitate an uninterrupted flow of sheep to the shearing board and from the board to the counting-out pens. At the same time the fleeces must flow forward to the skirting table, then to the wool-classer and wool press and on to the storage area.

Painted the same hue as the surrounding countryside is the rust-coloured shearing shed at Mardie station in the Pilbara of Western Australia. Sheds are generally centrally located, to keep to a minimum the distances the sheep must travel and thereby reduce dust collection.

Dominated by the historic Ferrier press and adorned with bale stamps, Bidgemia shearing shed is a shrine to times past. Sentimental owners of the Gascoyne property, Jane and Locky McTaggart, made the tough decision several years ago, on the back of destructive Cyclone Vance (they lost 35 windmills), to switch from sheep to cattle but wanted to preserve something of their wool heritage. 'This is proven sheep country and Bidgemia had produced a lot of good wool so we made the change with some reluctance,' says Jane. 'But with wool prices so depressed we were glum and pessimistic and financially unviable. The cattle have given us a new lease on life.' It took three years for them to adapt the property to suit cattle and to develop the herd to 8000 head.

Mustering and selling the wild goats that roam the Murchison district of Western Australia has kept Mount Narryer station afloat and paid for the private education of the McTaggart family's children. 'We sell from 3000 to 4000 goats a year to abattoirs or export depots and it's crucial to our financial survival; the goats constitute one-third of our income,' says Sandy McTaggart. So lucrative a natural resource are the goats that Sandy now counts them in with his 7000 sheep to determine the carrying capacity of his 200,000 hectare property. They are mustered two or three times a year using motorbikes and a plane, and taken to the station's shearing shed for drafting.

A vision splendid. It's July and shearing is about to get underway on Reola station in north-western New South Wales. Helicopters, gyrocopters, motorbikes and four-wheel-drives have been used to shepherd the mobs of sheep along 70 kilometres of fenced laneways that lattice the hopbush-studded plains. During the next three weeks the wool shorn from some 50,000 sheep will fill about 1500 bales. The modern shearing complex, with 16 stands in a horseshoe configuration, automatic wool baling, multilevel cover for up to 4500 sheep and drafting yard provision for 5000 sheep, epitomises the modern approach to shearing shed design, inspired by increased production costs and the quest for improved efficiency.

'They quieten right down when shedded; they're just like pets,' says Robert Watts of the 300 sheep rugged and housed on his New England property Nangoo. Under these salubrious conditions Robert and his wife Denise hope to produce perhaps five premium bales of ultrafine wool of under 14 microns. It means a little more work feeding the sheep twice daily and changing their rugs every 6 to 8 weeks, but the beautiful fleeces they cut — 'just like cotton wool' — contain only lanolin and minor contaminations. In September the sheep walk under cover to the shearing shed next door for further pampering. A single experienced shearer painstakingly defleeces the entire flock. 'Four board people will carefully prepare the wool for what we hope will be the exclusive Italian apparel market.'

Wool bale stamps tell the stories of a hundred shearings past at Balladonia station on the Nullarbor Plain. It remains a tough place to forge a living says current owner James Ferguson, who employs six people across Balladonia and adjoining Noondoonia stations. 'It's impossible to run these large properties like family farms and you have to be able to get on with your fellow workers,' he says. 'Getting good people to live out here is difficult and I'm trying to establish a career path for the younger ones.'

The Geelong firm Humble and Nicholson started manufacturing the famed Ferrier's lever press in 1861. As well as improving the methods of wool handling, the press became a highly ornate and richly decorated addition to the otherwise rudimentary woolshed. A surprising number of Ferrier's presses still loom large in shearing sheds across the country.

4

SHEARERS

It was once said that if the sheep station represented Australian autocracy, then the shearing shed was a true republic. Here, in 40-degree heat wrestling big wethers, every shearer is equal and judged only by their capacity for work. 'It's not hard work if you enjoy it and I always enjoyed the company,' says 58-year-old Braidwood blade devotee Artie Crisp.

Toil in the outback sheds at the dawn of the twentieth century inspired deep-seated traditions of Australian mateship and fierce independence — hallmarks of the profession that endure today, despite the growth of suburban shearing in the more closely settled parts of the country. Shearers continue to relish their freedom to choose where, for how long and how hard they will work and the rigour itself remains the same — eight hours of backbreaking slog until cut-out (the completion of shearing). Trials are underway for biological and mechanised techniques for defleecing our nation's flock but until they are perfected shearers are secure in Australian folklore.

Arthur 'Artie' Crisp (left) shows how it's done with blade shears on a tail-ender — the last sheep to be shorn — after machine shearing at Maybrook, near Braidwood. Artie learnt to shear at the age of 10 when he and his seven brothers routinely chased wild sheep along the Shoalhaven River, in some of the toughest river gorge country in the state. 'They were the woolly ones that wouldn't walk out or got left behind,' he said. 'We'd shear them and carry the wool out in a bag. Once we shore a sheep with five years' full fleece.' Few blade shearers survive today but Artie relishes the chance to do 'a few odd sheep for those hobby farmers who don't have electric sheds.'

Champion shearer Jackie Howe, immortalised in this bronze statue (opposite) in the main street of Blackall, set tongues wagging in 1892 when he shore 321 sheep in seven hours and 40 minutes using blade shears at nearby Alice Downs station. His astounding world record stood for fifty-five years. A year later, after switching to mechanical shears, he won the Wolseley medal for the highest tally — 237 ewes in one day at Barcaldine Downs station. Howe's second record, also set in 1892, was for shearing 1437 sheep in 44 hours — one standard working week. Patsy Adam-Smith, author of *The Shearers,* described Howe as 'The Bradman of the Shearing Board' and, true to form, he rang almost every shed he worked in. Legend has it he had hands the size of tennis rackets.

On the factory floor little has changed in decades, save for the introduction of the shearers' back aid and certain design modifications like the raised board (above, left) — this one at Denis and Marilyn Richmond's property Elmdon, near Cressy in Victoria. 'It improves the ease of handling the wool because the rouseabout doesn't have to bend to pick up the fleece and instead moves it straight across to the table for skirting and classing,' says Marilyn. Typical of practice on many smaller farms, the Richmond family all pitch in to shear the property's 3000 superfine merinos. Denis is the woolclasser, Marilyn works as the rousie and son Mark teams up with a couple of contract shearers. 'Our shearers come back year after year and have become good friends,' says Marilyn.

A moment of quiet contemplation as Wayne Small (above, right) checks his handpiece before commencing shearing at Coonong station, the first station bought by sheep magnate Samuel McCaughey in 1860, near Urana in southern New South Wales. The modern shearer's kitbag commonly contains a back aid, electric fan, handpiece, combs and cutters, screwdriver, oil can, brush and a 'wash-up tin' in which to put blunt combs and cutters. The shearer selects a comb according to the type of sheep being shorn and combs may vary not just from shed to shed but from mob to mob.

And so the dance begins (opposite). Good shearing has been described as a steady waltz — a series of synchronised movements and holds. Most modern domestic sheep breeds have lost their ancestors' ability to shed wool, and if not shorn regularly a sheep's fleece becomes so heavy that the animal is eventually unable to stand. Shearing takes place at different times around Australia, dictated by seasons, blowflies, lambing, market demands and the grower's own farm program.

FULL SIZE LETTER

Only the profession's best are contracted to shear the 400 to 500 sale rams at Rokeby Merino Stud each June (above) and they are paid princely for the privilege. 'Six months out from sale it's imperative that the rams are shorn evenly, without leaving any ridges, and the shearers are paid stud rates, plus an extra 30 per cent as an incentive to do a good job,' says Rokeby manager and stud master Andrew Calvert. The fleece weights and a current micron measurement are then available to potential purchasers in December at the on-property sale. Those who shear the 35-odd Rokeby and Castellon reserve rams each August are paid by the day, 'so there's no motivation to rush.' The care is warranted when you understand that total Tasmanian ram sales from these Merryman holdings amount to $500,000 a year and some of the elite rams are valued at $30,000 to 40,000 each.

In a scene reminiscent of Tom Roberts' 1890 painting *Shearing the rams*, modern-day shearers toil at Malboona station (opposite), north-east of Winton in central Queensland. Shearing is the busiest time on any property and in the sheds there's a prevailing spirit of comradeship spiked with competition. A century ago the man who shore the most sheep in a day was known as the ringer; the one who retained this title most consistently was the 'gun'. Many of the long-standing shearing records were set in Queensland, where the sheep were lighter and the wool less dense than in the southern states. But it wasn't enough to be fast; shearers also had to be clean and it was customary for some graziers to pay a premium at cut-out to the most meticulous shearer.

A stand of shearers (above). The team comprising (from left to right) Brian Argent, Kevin Adrians, John Ward, Stephen Malone, Bill Duffield, Ian Armstrong, Steve Kretschmer, Neal Argent and Ryan Jackson mainly works the sheds around Merredin, Western Australia, travelling no further than 120 kilometres. Historically shearers travelled over a vast area, on foot or bicycles, moving from one shed to another following the seasons. They were often away from home for months on end. Today, motorised transport has closed the distance between work and home and except in the truly isolated districts many are 'suburban shearers', returning to the comforts of home each night.

A window on an intriguing world as ram shearing progresses at Dunumbral station, near Collarenebri in northern New South Wales (opposite). Shearing used to last just four months of the year. Now it's conducted year-round but Australian flocks have declined and with them, the number of shearers. Just a decade ago 30,000 shearers were needed to shear Australia's 180 million sheep. Perhaps just 10,000 now tread the board and some regions are reporting shearer shortages. Most shearing these days is conducted under contract. The woolgrower engages a contractor to supply a team and pays the contractor an agreed fee. The contractor then pays the shearers the award rate (currently $1.78 per sheep shorn or 60 cents per head crutched) and usually organises workers compensation, superannuation and tax, issuing the shearers with monthly accounts.

Throwing the fleece (right). The value of a sheep's fleece is determined by the weight of clean wool produced and its average fibre diameter. Fineness has always commanded a premium. Young sheep generally produce the finest wool, which then increases in diameter until the animals are four or five years old, before resuming fineness but losing style as they age further. The areas around the shoulder, lower flank and legs typically yield the finest wool, while that on the britch — the back part of the sheeps upper leg — is the coarsest.

Like an increasing number of shearing contractors across Australia Darren Byrnes supplies buses to transport his teams from their Katanning homes to surrounding sheds in southern Western Australia. 'We start picking up at 6 a.m. and everyone's at work at the same time,' he says. 'We have a good old yack and tell a few jokes. They each pay $5 a day to go toward fuel and vehicle maintenance and if they sleep-in it costs them a carton of beer for the Friday afternoon cut-out.' One of his South Shear teams comprises (above: back row, left to right) Richard Durack, Peter Hitchcock, Tim Neale, Adam Thompson, Ross Wellstead and Jason King; (top — front row) Darren Byrne, dog Amber, Bree Smithson, little Carl Terry and Debra Terry.

Many of Australia's first and finest shearers were Aboriginal and Ray Cubby's team (bottom) continues this proud tradition around the sheds of northern New South Wales. Shearing at Willawillingbah were (back row, left to right) John Gibbs, Steve Rosenow, Ray Cubby, Wayne Gibbs, Tony Lamb, Terry Gibbs and (front row) Roger Cubby, Libby Busby, Ron Mason and Terry Cochrane — all but two of them Aboriginal. A shearer for thirty-four years, fifty-seven-year-old Ray reckons the practice of suburban shearing 'has buggered things up.' 'Before you were all mates out in the sheds; you'd stay out, have a few beers and tell a few yarns and you got to know the blokes better,' he says. 'It costs you a lot more to travel these days and I think that some of that mateship has been lost.'

A rest and a cuppa for Goodooga wool roller Ron Mason, who has worked with Ray Cubby's team for the past four years. Ron's five brothers, all in shearing, taught him how to throw a fleece using a blanket on the kitchen table and he started working in the sheds at age 15. After a 20-year absence he was welcomed back at age 56. 'It's a terrific job and the company is the main thing; there's a time to focus on your work and a time to share a joke,' he says. 'You go to work in the dark and come home in the dark and you earn your money. It's an honest living. I never forget that the way I treat the wool directly influences the prices the grower gets.'

Any job in the shed is demanding, but full marks must go to the wool presser, who in the days of the lever presses had one of the toughest assignments. Hydraulic presses have eased the burden somewhat, but bundling up the fleeces (top) — some weighing 8 kilograms — and loading them in the press remains hard work. Fleeces are pressed to as near as possible to 195 kilograms before the nylon bales are labelled and prepared for transport. It's a job that has engaged Terry Gibbs for thirty-five years in the sheds of northern New South Wales and he attributes his 'crook back' to the lever presses. 'It was tiring at the end of the day and your legs and arms would be sore but a little bit of sweat and hard work is good for you,' he says.

The hydraulic press (bottom) was not introduced until the 1960s. Operation of the earlier screw models, rack-and-pinion versions and lever presses required considerable strength and securing the fasteners was something of an artform.

An eye for detail and a passion for wool, legendary woolclasser Mervyn Shung (opposite) developed a formidable reputation during the 65 years he worked in sheds throughout New South Wales, 40 of them classing at Uardry station, where he is pictured. Now 87, he says his eyesight is failing but 'the old sheds and sheep never leave my mind.' A good classer relies on years of experience to assess a fleece's quality in seconds, considering its length, strength, colour, character (crimp) and condition. This assessment then determines how the wool is baled and sold. 'In my day you didn't have objective measurements and the classing depended on your own eyesight and feel and natural assessments,' he says. 'I think the old classers were pretty close to the machines in terms of accuracy. They have it easy now.'

There are few sheds around central Queensland that haven't at one time or another beckoned the National Grazing Services shearing teams organised by Noel Dawson, of Blackall. The national contracting service has some 2000 people on its books throughout Australia, 100 of them in Queensland, and last year at Malboona station, between Winton and Hughenden, this team (above) got through some 40,000 sheep in four weeks. But both sheep and shearer numbers are down in Queensland. Dry times, the shift to cattle and dingo attacks have depleted sheep flocks and Noel struggles to find people with the right work ethic for shearing. 'They work hard but they can earn good money (on average $1100 a week), you can be your own boss and be in charge of your own destiny,' he says. 'Shearing still has an appeal in the bush. The gun shearer is still looked up to and competition is rife for the high tallies.'

It was once customary for the shed expert to sharpen all the shearer's cutters and combs. Although the practice continues in some sheds most grind their own, as demonstrated by colleagues Alan Dick and George Wright (opposite, top) in the engine room at Dunumbral station. Sharp cutters, combs and well-maintained handpieces are the shearer's stock-in-trade and their kit might be valued at several thousand dollars. An old 'Bagman's Toast' stated: 'Shearer man like toast and butter, Wolseley comb and Lister cutter.' Such preferences prevail.

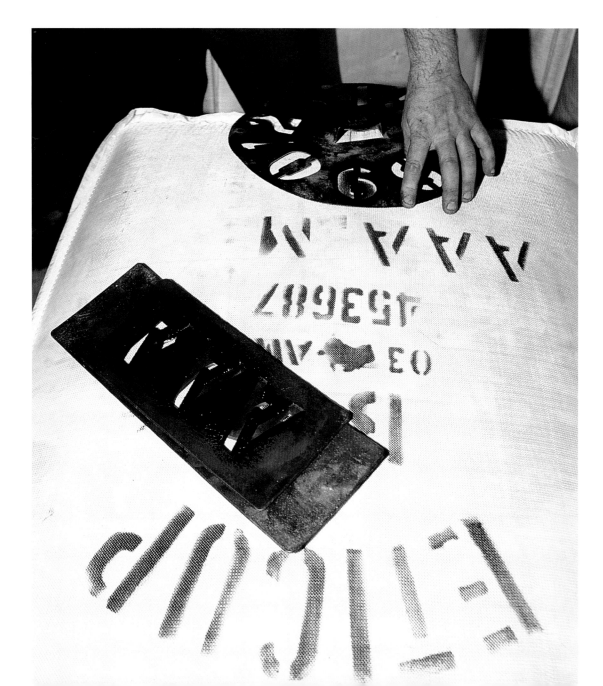

Reputations are on the line during a hotly-contested shearing competition at Wagin's Woolorama (above). Such competitions, held throughout the country year-round, instil a competitive spirit but, more importantly, help to maintain quality. 'It gives shearers the opportunity to test themselves against their colleagues on common ground and gives them an incentive to shear well,' says shearing judge of the Sports Shears national championships Bernie Walker. Competitors are judged for the speed and quality of their shearing on the board and out back (where the shorn sheep are carefully inspected), and compete for cash and gear prizes, plus the prestige of representing their country in international competition. Australia produces some of the world's best fine-wool shearers but the Kiwis reign supreme with the British breeds.

The operation of three hydraulic presses (Tim Hempel pictured stamping a bale) in the two-year-old Illira woolshed (opposite, top) is just one of the innovations that are already realising considerable productivity gains. The six-stand, smoke-free shed north of Hamilton in Victoria also features sloping floors in the catching pens, overhead fans and a large lunchroom. 'We took advice from an occupational therapist in designing the sloping floor because the major back injuries occur when the shearer twists the sheep on to the board,' says owner Mark Wootton. 'We haven't had a single back injury and we have shearers and shedhands clamouring to work here because it's a good shed with good amenities. All that translates into greater productivity because we get the best shearers.'

Every wool bale is core tested these days so stamping them — with the owner's brand, a description of wool, the classer's registered number and the bale number (opposite, bottom) — is not considered as important as it was in the past. However, even today such identification distinguishes one lot from another so that the bales can be catalogued on the showroom floor.

Design improvements in sheds are imperative if woolgrowers are to meet International Standards Organisation requirements, safeguard fleece quality and attract good shearing teams, according to Victorian woolgrower Mark Wootton. Jigsaw Farms have eight properties, supporting 35,000 sheep, and have invested in two new shearing sheds in recent years, this one at Illira (top) accommodating some 15,000 sheep during the February shearing. 'The old sheds are wonderful but many were a bugger to work in,' says Mark. 'Shearers want to be comfortable with good long runs, free of breaks, so they can work all day every day.'

Glen Newman drags a sheep from the pen at Coonong station, near Urana in New South Wales. Historian CEW Bean wrote in 1910 that a sheep had about five minutes of singular importance each year, 'the time it was handled by a shearer,' but securing good shearers is becoming increasingly difficult in the Riverina, especially with shearing concentrated in spring and early summer. 'We are losing shearers by the day; it's a hard job and there's easier work around,' says Coonong owner Tom Holt. 'The current shortage is a real worry. We're going to have to go from manual to mechanised shearing and if we don't in the next five or so years then we will have to find an alternative labour source outside Australia. When this current generation of older shearers retires it's going to be crunch time.'

The quick and the shed. A shearing team from Esperance take a breather at the Rawlinna station outcamp and show off their handiwork. Said one of the shearing culture: 'You live with them and share their worries, you know their problems, and you see them stripped down to the bare bones ... nothing gets in the way of who they are.' Dedication to mates and a strong work ethic remain the hallmarks of a profession that has changed little in a century. Friendly competition also endures and big tallies are a hot topic of discussion. Kevin Sarre's shearing record of 346 in one day, set in the western district of Victoria in 1965 with narrow combs, still stands. Under world record rules in December 2001 allowing the use of wide combs, Wellington shearer and Sports Shear Australia national champion Hilton Barrett shore 411 sheep in eight hours, adding six to the world record previously held by Nick Endacott of Uralla.

The lunchtime wash up on a hot March day at Harvey Park (right), near Coolac in southern New South Wales. Over eight days the team got through 8500 sheep in a shed that has changed little in one hundred years. 'It's one of the biggest away sheds we do,' says contractor Peter Kimber, of Bombala, whose father and two brothers were also shearers. 'We go all year round, but the ranks of the shearers are thinning. I teach learners because we have to try to keep our numbers up and get the smell of lanolin in their nostrils but a lot of the young fellas don't want to take on shearing; it's too bloody hard work.'

Smoko and Glen Newman (below) of Finley puts his feet up at Coonong station. The shearer's 10-hour day is usually divided into four 2-hour runs, broken by morning smoko (30 minutes), lunch (1 hour) and afternoon smoko (30 minutes). The down time is a chance to rest, fuel up, have a smoke and engage in a little friendly banter. Tocumwal contractor Mark Baldwin, who supplies this team, has clocked up 230,000 kilometres in his three-year-old ute travelling to sheds far and wide. 'We're lucky, we work most of the year, but we move around a lot to stay employed,' he says. 'Eight to 10 months of the year we camp out and that's all right provided the accommodation is okay. We used to have hut inspectors who helped maintain the quality of quarters but many have fallen into disrepair. A shearer's needs are pretty basic — good food, good accommodation and appreciation for their work. Shearers rave most about the cocky who acknowledges them when they arrive and thanks them when they leave.'

Comfortable blue dungarees, singlets and non-slip moccasins fashioned from felt remain the unofficial shearers' uniform and this team enjoying a hot cuppa at Bundy station are no exception. Contractor Noel Dawson says the influx of women has added colour to an otherwise drab shed. 'Women have brightened the whole industry up,' he says. 'You don't hear the swearing or see the behaviour you used to. Today's teams are much more professional.'

Freshly shorn sheep are plunge-dipped (right) in the traditional fashion at Raby station to ward against lice, itch-mites and blowflies leading in to summer. Raby manager Ashley Bell prefers the more laborious plunge dip over backline applications and shower dips because he says it affords better coverage. After being pushed through the trough the sheep are let drain in a holding pen for about 10 minutes before being released. Blowflies remain one of the sheep's greatest foes and lay their eggs on dirty or moist wool. The maggots emerging from the eggs eat the sheep's flesh and wool, causing the sheep to be flyblown. The merino is susceptible to flystrike because of its dense fleece, its wrinkly skin and abundant body secretions.

When sheep are in the yards at Malboona station, north-east of Winton (opposite, left), it's a prime opportunity to mark, mules and drench at the one time. Lamb-marking contractors remove tails, then mules — the removal, by operation, of folds of skin either side of the buttocks, leaving an area on which wool doesn't grow. This controversial practice, usually performed when lambs are 3 to 8 months old, is designed to keep the sheep's rear cleaner so they are less likely to be flystruck and proponents say it gives the sheep lasting protection. At Malboona the mulesing is sometimes also followed by drenching.

Stripes are all the rage at Yeadon station in the Riverina, north-east of Hay (opposite, right). In this low rainfall belt — on average 355 millimetres a year — the sheep are relatively free of disease and need only be sprayed for lice. Elsewhere shorn sheep are also drenched against parasites and worms. Backline applications were introduced as an alternative to dipping but the sheep must be treated within 24 hours of shearing. 'Backline applications' are chemicals administered with a gun-like applicator along the sheeps backbone.

In his book *On the Wool Track*, C E W Bean wrote that a shearers' cook had to be good at two things: baking bread and fighting. In times past, when a worker's daily allowance comprised one-tenth of a sheep and two pounds of bread, the cook had to sustain and cajole up to 90 hungry people camping out at remote sheds for often a month or more. It was their job to plan menus, order foodstuffs and then cook up a variety of wholesome meals using problematic wood stoves and without refrigeration. Tempers sometimes flared when it came to the tucker, while kitchen hygiene and physical altercations between cooks and shearers are the stuff of legend.

Part chef, part psychologist and part magician, the shearers' cook continues to carry an enormous responsibility today for maintaining the morale and strength of shearing staff. While suburban shearing has done some cooks out of a job, others still roam the backblocks with a car full of gear, mentally compiling *101 Imaginative Ways with Mutton* and conjuring up hunger-sating dishes from limited ingredients. It's a job that demands patience, mastery with leftovers, lashings of good humour and a thick skin. And those without butchering and wood-chopping skills need not apply.

Rawlinna gardener–handyman–butcher Michael 'Micky' Sprigg (left) butchers a sheep for shearers' tucker at the station's outcamp in south-eastern Western Australia. A steady supply of mutton feeds up to 14 shearers during the two solid months of shearing from February to April; the common ration is one sheep to 10 workers. Mutton is commonly supplied by the woolgrower at a low-agreed rate per kilo and is therefore economical. In describing his experience as a cook Roger McDonald has written: 'It became a mutton-a-thon in the kitchen, a carnivorous race. Now there was meat everywhere, joints baked specially to use in other dishes, two legs and a shoulder every night-time ...'

Baked vegies and surprise, surprise — a leg of mutton — tempt diners at Chez Haddon Rig (below). 'It's not flash and it's not gourmet, but most shearers say they put on weight while I'm cooking,' says Fiona Pilley, who has been catering for the team here, sometimes numbering 35 workers, for twelve years. 'Most like plain, basic meals but plenty of it. It's mutton, mutton, mutton but they never seem to tire of it. You could go to the effort of cooking things differently but they're bent over all day and many things don't agree with them and they don't want the food repeating on them. The guys I cook for are very appreciative. They pay me, so they have the right to sack me, but that's never happened.'

It's the cook's responsibility to prepare three hot main meals and two smokos each day and contend with all the washing-up during a shift that commonly stretches from 5 am to 9 pm. Their patience and ingenuity is frequently tested by poorly equipped kitchens used just once a year, so many carry their own equipment (including toasters, mix-masters, frypans and portable fridges) and some specialist supplies. Longer-lasting foodstuffs and modern kitchen appliances have made things easier but for cooks like Terry Louk, pictured (opposite) at Malboona station, it remains a thankless task. Typical of the scorn heaped on cooks, a cheeky epitaph reportedly read: 'Here lies the body of Watty the Guy; He cooked for ten shearers and nine of them died.'

Few other episodes in shearing history have had as profound an influence as the wide comb affair of the early 1980s. It tested the strength of the unions, pitted shearer against shearer and spawned a raft of workplace changes.

The dispute began with the introduction of wide combs (88–96 millimetres wide) in 1982 that enabled shearers to shear more sheep than with the narrow gear (about 60–64 millimetres). The unions opposed the introduction, contesting that Australian shearers would lose their jobs to New Zealanders (who already used wide combs, along with West Australians), that shearing quality would suffer and that the increased output of shearers would place other shed staff under pressure.

Australian shearers were split between those who favoured and those who rejected the wide combs. The ones who chose to continue working throughout the protracted strike action sometimes required protection.

The unions launched an expensive but eventually unsuccessful court case and wide combs were adopted in 1983 without huge effects on the industry. Many shearers, out of pocket and out of faith, felt a bitterness towards the union that persists today and some blame the union's reaction to wide combs for declining union membership. Says one old-timer: 'I haven't seen the union organiser since the wide combs came out. The wide combs broke down our rules and conditions and eroded the union's power. I think the union might have given up. 'Says managing director of National Grazing Services, Noel Dawson: 'The unions fell out of favour during the wide-comb dispute and they haven't been able to regain ground.'

Before unionisation shearers worked according to terms laid down by the cocky in a signed agreement. 'It's almost a workplace agreement that exists between the shearer and the contractor these days and it works very well,' says Noel. 'No contracts are signed but there seems to be greater trust between the two parties.'

Greame Tyers clearly demonstrates the advantage of the wide comb handpiece holds over the narrow. The difference was only about two and a half centimetres but it turned the shearing industry on its head.

Belly: about 4 blows towards the groin to remove the belly wool in one piece;

Crutch: 2 blows down through the crutch;

First hind leg: working up the inside of the first hind leg in about 4 to 5 blows;

Top knot (the wool between a sheep's ears): 2 blows;

Neck: 4 blows.;

First shoulder: 3 to 4 blows;

Long blow: a series of about 5 sweeps that run from the rump right up to the back of the head;

Over the head and around the shoulder. (3 blows);

Last quarter: 6 blows. The fleece finally comes away in one piece, the wool held together by connecting fibres and natural grease.

Shed guns routinely shear more than 200 sheep a day in an artful demonstration of technique and rhythm. Various styles of shearing have been adopted over the years in an attempt to streamline the process and ensure that the fleece comes off quickly and cleanly. Essentially, the shearer begins by getting his or her body and the sheep in the correct starting position. Keeping the comb flat on the sheep's skin the shearer uses its full width to take long blows in the following sequence.

5

PORTRAIT GALLERY

A beautiful fibre, with unique properties, wool inspires a special commitment from all those linked together along the value chain. Author, stud breeder and woolgrower Charles Massy has likened the breeder to an artist, 'working on a 50-year canvas' but few artists could tolerate such unpredictable working conditions — most notably, capricious global market forces and environmental conditions. 'Sheep breeding requires resilience, certitude and patience,' Charles says. 'The breeder must have multidisciplinary skills and a long-term view, be prepared to make a lot of mistakes to learn, and yet remain true to their original vision.'

EW Cox wrote in *The Evolution of the Australian Merino*, published in 1936: 'A great sheep stud is something like a power station. You cannot see the process by which electricity is made inside the hooded generators, but you can watch its effects in the life and work of a whole community. In a similar way the stud's methods remain its secret; but its triumphs shine abroad, and its standard products infuse life into the economy of a nation.'

An innovator in sheep breeding and wool marketing, Jim Maple-Brown (right) reflects on his contributions to the industry with a mixture of pride and sadness. He's proud of the easy-care Fonthill breed he developed at Springfield — the merino stud near Goulburn founded by his great-grandfather William Pitt Faithful in 1838 — and that he helped inspire the now common practices of selling by sample and description and selecting stock by objective measurement. His marketing strategy — Fibre Direct, now managed by Wesfarmers Landmark and adopted by hundreds of growers to establish a brand name for quality-assured wool is also a source of satisfaction — sees wool sold direct to the Italian wool processing and weaving mills. But he remains frustrated by the inherent conservatism of the industry. 'It has not appreciated the worth of a lot of the research it has financed,' he says. 'We have thrown away opportunities to create a truly competitive environment that encourages innovative people and that's a tragedy.'

Charlie Massy (opposite) spent six years meticulously documenting the evolution of our wool industry to produce *The Australian Merino* — considered by many the industry bible. The weighty tome punctured many long-held myths and highlighted the way in which Australian sheep breeders revolutionised an entire global industry by 'reconstructing an animal to suit new industrial practices.' At his property Severn Park, near Cooma, history is in abundance, like this wall of a sheepfold built by Chinese miners in the 1860s, but so, too, is progressive thinking. 'The future lies in innovation,' says Charlie, whose main business is selling Soft Rolling Skin genetics to clients nationally. 'We have to produce superior performing fibres for our customers at an efficient cost with environmental sustainability superimposed on top.'

The 7000 sheep that form the heart of the Bullamalita Merino Stud, just south-east of Goulburn, have been under quarantine for Ovine Johne's disease for a year. It has been a costly experience for owner Bob Peden, pictured (right) with worker Neville Klower, but one that he is ready to talk about. 'If you murder someone you can be out in ten years but with this it's a lifetime ban; you don't trade out of it,' he says. 'I believe it will cost us $500,000 a year but how do you put a value on a stud that's been running for eighty years?' Bob hasn't actually lost any sheep to Johne's and is permitted to sell stock to other infected breeders — now numbering 152 in the Goulburn Pastures Protection Board alone — but must use slaughter-only yards for meat sales. He remains philosophical. 'The threat is not as serious as some people will have you believe. We've been fortunate in that those farms infected in the initial stage, nine years ago, were considered lepers. People are much more accepting now. I'd like to think that we will beat the disease, not that it will beat us.'

Third generation sheep grazier Graham Brown (opposite) proudly poses with elite ram Sweet 16 (so named because he cost $16,000 and grew 16-micron wool) used for artificial insemination on Reola station, in the western division of New South Wales. The Brown family have pioneered many innovative farming practices on this 174,150 hectare station, which Graham has described as a 'light on the hill for future generations of western wool producers.' The station's centrepiece is a state-of-the-art shearing complex that ranks among the largest in the world, with a floor area of 3000 square metres. The visionary Browns first started using helicopters in 1981 and gyrocopters were added to their armoury in 1988. Solar-powered subartesian-bore pumps were introduced in 1985 and up to 3000 of Reola's best ewes are now artificially inseminated each year. One of Graham's favourite quotes is 'Quality is never an accident. It represents the wise choice of many alternatives.'

Egelabra Merino Stud is something of a rarity — a parent stud that has maintained a pure genetic strain of Spanish merinos throughout one hundred years of breeding. The stud has about 10,000 breeding ewes on three properties around Warren that are direct descendants of the merino sheep bred by the Reverend Samuel Marsden and sells about 2200 of its versatile stud rams annually to growers from Longreach to Tasmania and Western Australia. General manager Cam Munro, pictured holding daughter Alice with his wife Kate in the office, describes it as a 'family-oriented' operation that provides employment opportunities for up to eight jackeroos each year.

The property Belltrees has been in the White family for six generations and today Judy White is proud to call home the ornate 54-room homestead — 'a legacy of the wool boom years.' By the end of the nineteenth century the Hunter Valley estate was a community to some 250 permanent residents, replete with 62 buildings, including a church, entertainment halls, 18 boundary riders' houses and school. The grand homestead was completed in 1908 at a cost of £11,000 and impresses with its fine joinery and decorative silver-leaf ceilings. High labour costs and the proliferation of burrs and grass seeds have seen the White family's move away from wool production into cattle, polo ponies and tourism. 'But we want to maintain the property as a part of Australia's rural heritage,' says Judy.

A former board boy, wool classer, fine-wool sheep grower and now wool consultant, Ross Tully has enjoyed an association with wool that stretches back sixty-five years. Thanks to his wife Peg's talent for making detailed wool art, entirely from naturally-coloured wool, he can still get the fibre between his fingers from time to time. Ross, 82, was instrumental in bringing Japanese wool buyers to the New England district in the early 1980s and in promoting the district's wool overseas. 'In the past woolgrowers would grow wool and it was sent to Newcastle or Sydney and they had no idea what happened after that,' he says. 'It was difficult to get wool buyers or manufacturers to visit the bush.'

The man behind the Swanwool Scouring Company in Fremantle and seven other wool scours nationally — Bill Hughes — was at one time the biggest scouring operator in Australia. 'Many of the overseas scouring plants were damaged during World War Two and processors reverted back to scouring in the nation of origin,' he says. 'Our scoured wool was sold to every country in the world.' After riding to some considerable wealth on the sheep's back during the scouring renaissance, Bill invested in Australian art, including Arthur Streeton's *Golden Summer*. He sold the painting to the National Gallery several years ago but cherishes a copy that hangs in his Fremantle home.

The panoramic views from the shearing shed meal room at Heatherlea rarely fail to enliven superfine wool-grower Brian Fraser, a sixth generation wool producer who has been at it himself for fifty years. High rainfall, natural and improved pastures — and some dedicated sheep-breeding — have combined to produce excellent wool-growing conditions here on the New South Wales–Victorian border. Brian and Mary Fraser's Tallangatta property runs 9000 sheep that produce fleeces in the realm of 17 microns. Brian is a federal councillor on the Australian Superfine Woolgrowers' Association and a shareholder in the Australian Wool Network, comprising Australian woolgrowers and Italian and Japanese processors. About 17 per cent of Australian woolgrowers produce superfine fleeces and these fleeces constitute about 29 per cent (500,000 bales) of national wool production (4 million bales).

The scenic coastline behind Dunsborough, in Western Australia, is every bit as beautiful as the superfine fleeces produced by Andrew d'Espeissis, pictured at right with (right to left) his wife Clare and children Emily, James and Freya. The 900 hectare property sustains 1500 merinos — sheep that have become Andrew's abiding passion. 'It's the pursuit of quality that drives me, but that takes time,' he says. 'Sheep breeding is an evolving process and you can't afford to chop and change to follow market trends. It demands patience and a belief in the direction you're taking; then you have to hope your belief is supported by market demand.'

Stud breeder Wally Merriman (right) oversees one of the greatest fine-wool studs in Australia — Merryville at Boorowa in the south-western slopes of New South Wales. Combined with the Rokeby holding in Tasmania, the stud has over 2500 ram and ewe clients and posts sales of 1600 rams a year. Wally says he targets the Italian 19.5 micron and higher market, with some of his broader wools going to Korea and Japan. 'Our wool is a little dusty to get the best Italian money,' he says. 'The message, emphatically, from our wool buyers is that they want traditional wool types. The fine end of the clip produces the best fabric; it absorbs dye more readily and has more elasticity in the weave.'

Rugs are de rigueur on the New England property owned by Greg Munsie (opposite, at right) and his brother Peter but the fashion is on the wane. The brothers were the first in the New England region to rug their superfine wool sheep fifteen years ago, at Kelvin Vale just north-east of Uralla, and up until about three years ago it paid off. The nylon rugs help exclude dust and vegetable matter, prevent fleece weathering and the sheep cut marginally heavier fleeces averaging 16.1 microns but it's labour intensive and expensive. 'We have 500 rugged sheep and they need to be checked every week,' says Peter. 'Then the costs in the shed are double that of ordinary sheep; our shearer does just 120 a day and we take our time with the preparation and classing of the fleeces. The premium we're paid is below the cost of production.' The Munsies persist with the rugging because it helps ram sales — some 150 a year.

The Cormo breed developed in 1960 by Tasmanian Ian Downie — initially from crossing stud Corriedale rams with selected superfine Saxon merino ewes — has been controversial. It was the first Australian sheep breed to be established on objective measurement rather than stud principles. 'One has to use the eye to make sure undesirable characteristics don't creep in but touch and tickle is never as good as objective measurement,' Ian says. 'The attractiveness of the breed is in the technology of the system; there's less variation in the fibre which makes it more economical to process.' The Cormo sheep is noted for its fast growth rates, high fertility and high wool yield and is now found in Belgium, Italy, Japan, China, the United States, Argentina, Canada and Sweden.

Pride in his rural heritage continues to motivate Bob McFarland of Oxley station. His great-great-grandfather imported the first Rambouillet ram to Australia in the 1860s, by the name of Matchless, and the family's merino stud takes his regal name. The King of Spain is reputed to have worn underwear made from this kind of wool and in more recent times the McFarlands have been developing sheep based on Rambouillet genetics using the Soft Rolling Skin gene. 'It's a very exciting challenge and I'm rekindling something I've long held a passion for,' says Bob, who has also put his faith in artificial insemination, joining 3400 ewes in the stud's first natural cycle.

'If they can live anywhere, why not here?' was the ardent belief that inspired Judith McGeorge in her determined efforts to produce traditional fine wool 175 kilometres north-west of Quilpie, in western Queensland. Today, Lynwood is one of only two properties in the district producing this wool type — a success story that began with the introduction of fine-wool rams in 1980. 'People claimed they would never cut enough wool and that the conditions were too harsh but this has all changed with the realisation that it can be done,' says Judith, pictured handling a ram with son Garry and his children Alexander and Emma Kate McGeorge. 'In my book, after the collapse of the wool market, you had to have quality or it wasn't worth growing wool. And we had the right country to produce fine wool — soft mulga, Mitchell grass and Mitchell downs.' The 'mentally absorbing' task of breeding is to Judith a 'quest for perfection.' And the rewards? 'When you see the first drop of new lambs and they're a genetic improvement and when you look in those bins in the shearing shed and see glorious, bright, soft-handling wool.'

Typical of many contemporary sheep farmers, Wooleen owners Brett (pictured) and Helen Pollock have diversified to supplement farm income. 'We bought the place twelve years ago and within six months the price of wool had crashed,' Brett says. 'It's been a very tough decade and it's our station-stay business that's got us through. But we love this place and we love wool. We had a firm belief that wool would come back and it has. Tourism has enabled us to run less sheep (now 14,000) and look after the rangelands better.' The Murchison landscape, resplendent with kangaroos and a myriad birds, and the hospitality the Pollock's extend, has proved very popular among international visitors.

A locust plague in 2001 was near disastrous for South Australian woolgrower Kerry Modystach (above) and dry times have taken their toll on his property Woollahra, near Wilmington. But he is increasingly hedging his bets against uncertain wool prices by pre-selling his clip or taking out Macquarie Futures. 'It's good to know what wool price you're going to get, for bank negotiations, budgetary and other planning,' he says, 'and if wool prices fold then you're locked in.' The Macquarie Futures option pays growers a figure based on the average value for wool in northern South Australia.

Buddie Wagstaff (opposite) was a babe in arms when her mother brought her home to Thornleigh station in central western Queensland and she hasn't strayed far ever since. She has largely handed over the running of Thornleigh and nearby Moorlands to her two daughters Wendy and Lindy but maintained the property virtually single-handedly for many years after the death of her husband Mike in 1969. She's watched cattle and dingoes slowly encroach on traditional sheep country. 'I'm definitely not tempted to switch to cattle,' she says. 'I don't think this country is right for cattle. In bad times sheep will battle on when you'd be looking for agistment for cattle.' Buddie, now 73, lists better blowfly dips and the introduction of earthmoving equipment as some of the better innovations of her lifetime.

Angus Deane (left) lived on the stock routes of northern New South Wales for more than a year when drought gripped his Queensland station Malboona in 1996–97. He had 40,000 head spilt between three droving crews and eight agisted paddocks and didn't lose a single sheep. 'We've had twelve years of shit wool prices and eleven years of drought, but that's life,' he says. 'You get a good year here and there; we just haven't been getting our share of the good ones lately.' Malboona's cover of Mitchell and Flinders grasses provides excellent sheep feed but the average annual rainfall is just 430 millimetres. While many of his neighbours have moved to cattle he remains adamant that it is better suited to sheep. 'Cattle will die when sheep are still mud-fat in this country; the cattle blokes are forever stocking and destocking,' Angus says. 'The seasons are your biggest hurdle out here.'

The grandeur of the Bungaree station homestead (opposite) speaks of another, more prosperous era when wool was king, the stud was one of Australia's largest and most influential, and the property sustained 100,000 sheep. Today George and Sally Hawker run just 3000 head on the station established by his great-grandfather George in 1841, 12 kilometres north of Clare in South Australia. As Charlie Massy says in *The Australian Merino*: 'the Bungarees were bred in tough country for tough conditions, and constituted the largest framed sheep in Australia, with some of the strongest wool … the Bungaree sheep were great survivors, highly fertile, docile and productive as well.' George's successes gave rise to a virtual village and during shearing the station employed up to 100 people. Economic factors have seen the present-day Hawkers restrict woolgrowing to focus instead on cereal crops, cattle and deer farming on their arable lands. 'You have to be adaptive; you can't live in the past,' says George.

The Tasman is but a short divide when it comes to sheep and New Zealanders have played an integral part in the evolution of the Australian wool industry. Large Kiwi teams have supplemented the Australian work force during peak times and were among the first to use wide combs in Australia, having pioneered their use in New Zealand. Some say they have also brought an improved attitude to shearing — a willingness to shear sheep free of political influence.

'A lot of the Australian shearers initially saw the Kiwis as a threat, and the union encouraged them to think that way,' says New Zealand-born Barry Hammond, who was physically threatened and consistently harassed when he joined the first shearers to use wide combs in Queensland in 1985. 'But Australia wouldn't get its sheep shorn without the influx of New Zealand shearers, even today, between those that come over for the season and those that have permanently settled here.'

But while Kiwis have been credited with the introduction of wide combs, which speeded up shearing by up to 30 per cent, increased shearers' incomes and reduced shearing costs, some divisions run deep. A proportion of Australian shearers remain critical of those New Zealand shearers who have 'put up with anything and done anything to make a buck' — often against union guidelines — then smartly returned home. Many others have made good lives here over the decades and as shearers and contractors are mainstays of the industry.

Developing a uniform strategy for workplace safety and quality assurance in wool handling have been the major goals of champion shearer and shearing instructor Samson Te Whata (above, left). The director of Shearpak, a training company based in Dubbo, Samson has developed a grid system for movement on the shearing floor that he hopes will safeguard shearers and wool handlers from injury and lead to more efficient wool handling. 'Shearers have traditionally learnt the trade through word of mouth but we have to be more precise to compete well,' he says. 'The workers compensation deficit in Australia in rural agriculture is $2 billion and shearing makes up a large part of that. We are providing common ground for workplace training, a uniform measure of efficiency and liaison between administration and the cutting edge.'

New Zealand-born Barry Hammond (left) earnt the wrath of the Australian Workers Union and spent six days in Charleville jail in 1991 and 1992 for breaching the Queensland Shearing Award but it hasn't deterred him from challenging the might of Australia's shearers' unions. He and his wife Moera took over a shearing run at Charleville in 1988 and today run Troubleshooters Available — a contract labour hire business with hundreds of shearing workers on its books in Queensland and New South Wales that annually shear about 500,000 sheep. They have a direct agreement with pastoralists to supply a shearing team and then subcontract the work to team members, who have individual contracts. 'It delivers more efficient shearing to the cockies and the shearers,' says Barry. 'The team members either use a group income protection scheme or have their own cover, they're not subject to the rigid rules of the award and for the cockies there's no threat of union action or other complications that come with having employees.'

Retired Maori shearing contractor Clem McHaure (opposite, right) answered an advertisement in a Western Australian newspaper in 1969 and became one of the first New Zealanders to shear in that state in a new wave of trans-Tasman worker migration that has been a feature of the industry since colonial times. It was a career that took him all over Australia until his retirement to Hamley Bridge in South Australia.

'Everyone, including my relatives, was telling me I was mad but now they're telling me I'm lucky; I just hope the luck holds out,' says James Ferguson, who in 1998 invested heavily in the adjoining Nullarbor stations Balladonia and Noondoonia. A decade of poor seasons and poor prices, coupled with uncertainty over the tenure of Western Australian pastoral leases, gave James his opportunity to re-enter the wool industry after a fifteen year absence and he's now running 25,000 sheep on 300,000 hectares. 'We have been amazingly blessed with three record years in a row and I trust that it's the beginning of a new era of profitability. I'm hoping to be here for the rest of my life.' Still, with the average paddock measuring 8 kilometres by 8 kilometres, with visibility down to a few hundred metres, just getting a clean muster remains a fundamental challenge.

After fourty-one years on the payroll at Mungadal station Bryant Hunt finds it hard to stay away. Despite pseudo-retirement he continues to act as the stud's representative, helping clients with ram selection and classing, and prepares the Mungadal sale and show stock as well as helping out with ram wool testing and mothering up. 'It's quite good to go out there, to get out in the open and mix with the boys,' says Bryant, who is also a show steward and judge. Now part of the Twynam Pastoral Company, the Mungadal stud was founded in 1865 and has a reputation for breeding large-framed, heavy cutting sheep that produce medium wools. Bryant has outlasted three owners and several managers.

A fine touch. Wool classer Kevin Mahler (above) at work at Malboona station.

Bidgemia stationhand Des Lumby (opposite), a former shearer, has shorn in Italy and the United States, where he was once arrested for overstaying his visa. When Bidgemia ran sheep he was a regular on the board and he moved from shed to shed following the shearing in the Gascoyne region. The station historically employed 20 to 30 station hands but the work force has declined with the changeover to cattle; now the McTaggarts employ about 10 people seasonally.

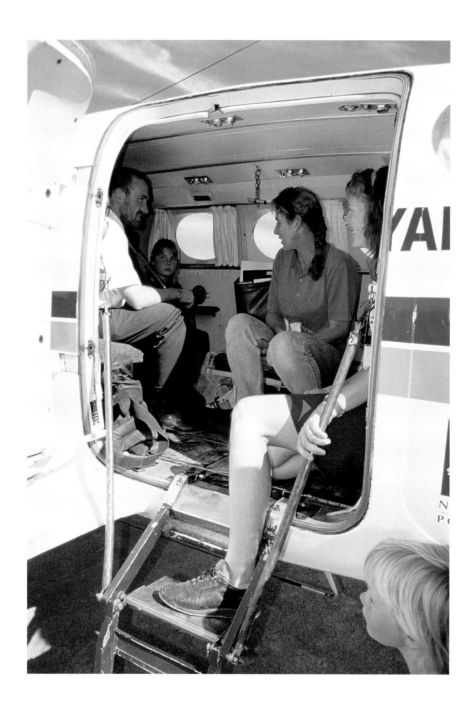

Royal Flying Doctor Serivce of Australia's clinic on the airstrip at Moonera station on the Nullarbor Plain. Jo Wood with daughter Diane sit inside the plane, with Dr Donal Watters and flight nurse Christine Speirs. Matthew Wood is looking on.

Former stationhand Corey Follezani and yardsman of twenty-two years Kevin Reynolds share a joke in the Bidgemia station workshop, east of Carnarvon. The contraction of the station's work force in recent years is typical of the social shift throughout Australia as sheep have been displaced by cattle. 'Once the shearers and their families go the communities contract,' says Jane McTaggart. 'When everyone was shearing around here and there were three or four big shearing teams we'd have footy and cricket matches in the [Gascoyne] Junction. The big shearing runs and shearers attracted money to the area. It's an era gone. Once the community dwindles you lose families, schools and other facilities and end up attracting itinerant single labour instead.'

Almost 1900 stud names and 60,000 individual working dogs are registered with the Working Kelpie Council of Australia — and that's not counting the many border collies and countless unregistered dogs nipping at the heels of the national flock. A dedicated handler will train a dog over a period of up to three years — a commitment that demands patience, diligence and communication on the part of handler and dog alike.

Dogs bred by Mary McCrabb, of Avenpart Kelpie Stud, have been exported to 19 countries, including New Zealand, Kuwait, Norway, Sweden, South Korea, Iran, the United States, the United Kingdom and Argentina, where they work cattle, deer, goats and pigs as well as sheep. The Riverina stud, founded in 1962, successfully pioneered the first export of kelpie semen from Australia, to Scotland in 1996. 'I look for a natural working ability at a young age, sound conformation and good temperament in my dogs,' says Mary, whose family continue to use dogs extensively for mustering, yard and shed work on their 16,500 hectare merino stud. 'They also work our cattle and kelpies are in demand throughout Australia for cattle work.'

An eye for talent. Although semi-retired from dog breeding, Byn Dinning continues to trial with one of his more successful charges, Gallpens Champ. Byn started breeding and training border collies from his Naracoorte home in 1947 and went on to represent his state in sheepdog trials across Australia and the Tasman. He estimates he has bred about 2000 collies during his career, some of which now roam American sheep ranches. 'I like the collie,' Byn says. 'The kelpie breeders will have their own view, but I think the collies are more tractable and have a better temperament.' All but a handful of the sheepdogs trialled throughout Australia are border collies.

Kelpie breeder of twenty-eight years' experience, Nancy Withers with bitch Pomanda Idgee and puppy at the Withers family property near Naracoorte in South Australia. 'In these times of a dwindling rural workforce, the working dog has become even more important,' says Nancy, the principal of the Pomanda Working Kelpie Stud and author of *Your Kelpie*. 'A good dog saves hours of labour, fuel costs and vehicle repairs and improves the efficiency of moving your sheep.' Nancy believes that a kelpie shouldn't be taught to work, but should simply be taught obedience. 'The working style is natural; it should be bred into the dog,' she says. 'I have tried to retain in my dogs traits that the stockmen of old valued: dogs which think for themselves and shepherd sheep in a strategic manner in the paddock and yards rather than drive them. Good kelpies, in general, don't like or need too many commands and I'm particularly interested in teaching others about the psychology of the breed and how to work with them.'

When he's not training sheepdogs Rex Johnson works as the shire animal control officer ('a fancy title for dog catcher') at Blackall, in central Queensland. A breeder since 1957 and former horse breaker–drover–musterer, he only recently established his stud Rexton but his pups have been dispatched to every state and territory of Australia with the exception of the Northern Territory. 'I have never advertised. I've just bred the dogs for myself and sold the rest of the litter; word always gets around,' he says. 'In my view the kelpies are the hardiest of the sheepdog breeds and the most versatile, especially on a station, because you don't need a special dog for a special job.' His dogs, he says are very loyal companions but a 'little shy of strangers'.

History is in abundance at Kemminup Farm, 12 kilometres north-east of Kojunup in Western Australia, where Doreen and Trevor Bignell cherish an original wattle and daub shearing shed. The property was first settled by the Bignell family in 1900 and now, in addition to running 7000 fine-wool sheep, they operate a 4.5-star homestay business. The historic shed is made of wattle sticks bound together with red clay dug from a nearby well and now houses a collection of old bottles, farm machinery and equipment and tools.

It's a long road ahead for certified organic woolgrower Wayne Kupke but he's already seeing benefits to his sustainable land and sheep management practices. He applies no chemicals to his sheep or his pastures 12 kilometres south-west of Wudinna, in southern South Australia, choosing instead to add minerals to water troughs or administer mineral supplements orally to sheep in a bid to correct the mineral imbalances in the soil. His 900 head of sheep are healthy, his soil quality is vastly improved and he takes pleasure in contributing to better district land protection in what is a marginal rainfall area. But finding markets for organic wool is another matter. While he is paid premiums for his organic grain he is yet to uncover an organic wool market and sells just 4 to 6 sheep a month (as organic mutton) to a Port Lincoln buyer. Still, he remains undaunted. 'If we can learn to balance the soil more economically that will be great,' he says. 'Those using artificial fertilisers are getting the yields but it's at the cost of their soils.'

Direct descendants of the Royal Spanish flock roam the lush pastures of John and Vera Taylor's property Winton, north-west of Campbell Town in Tasmania. Founded in 1835 it is the oldest continuously owned family stud in Australia, our only true superfine merino parent stud and home to some of the purest Saxon merinos to be found anywhere in the world — direct descendants of those given to the Elector of Saxony by the King of Spain in 1765. 'In recent times we have marketed our wool under the brand name Escorial (the name of the Spanish King's palace) and woolgrowers using our bloodlines have had an exclusive arrangement to supply the world's leading Italian suit manufacturer Brioni,' says John.

Big deals still go down in the 'ram buyer's room' at Uardry station, decades after the influential Riverina stud was established. And regally watching over the proceedings is Uardry 01, the 1932 Sydney Royal Grand Champion strong-woolled ram and inspiration for the shilling coin minted six years later — an honour he held until decimal currency was introduced in 1966. 'He was known as Hallmark because he was such an outstanding animal,' says Uardry manager Chris Bowman, great-great-grandson of the stud's founder Charles Mills. 'He had a sirey outlook, tremendous head, great length of body and a good cover of wool.' Today, the stud sells 1600 rams annually and remains one of the largest in Australia.

The inherently conservative wool industry prides itself on time-honoured traditions and is not noted for its design innovations, with a few significant exceptions. The development of mechanised shearing machines has been underway since the 1960s, with several models now in commercial use. Woolgrowers in the eastern states and Western Australia are also now using Bioclip, a biological defleecing method that involves injecting sheep with a natural protein (Epidermal Growth Factor) that weakens the wool fibres near the skin. The sheep is then covered with a protective netting (fleece retention net) and after 36 hours a natural break occurs in the fleece and the fleece can be removed.

But until these new techniques for defleecing are perfected and commercial applications refined, the shearer will reign supreme — more often than not supported by a Warrie back aid slung under his arms.

The Gum Hill Wool Harvesting and Husbandry System, pictured here with pioneer designer Lance Lines, is about to go into commercial production and the Lines family is confident it will halve wool harvesting costs. 'The machine vastly improves the occupational health and safety of shearing and results in far superior wool harvesting by enabling the shearer to take off the good fleece wool faster,' says Lance's son Glan. 'Because the shearer has total control, smooth flat controlled strokes give a higher real yield by eliminating second cuts and skin cuts are virtually eliminated.' The sheep is secured on a revolving belt table, immobilised using electrical impulses, and then shorn by a shearer standing on an ergonomic mat. The unit is mobile and sheep can be crutched, marked, tagged and vaccinated at the same time to minimise mustering costs.

Shearers throughout the country have Warren Hambley (left) to thank for the aid that dramatically reduces their back strain. A former shearer with a nagging back injury himself, Warren developed the aid in 1983 and has sold nearly 100,000 around the world, with an 80 per cent take-up among Australian shearers. Retailing for between $80 and $212, the aid works by immobilising the back, relaxing ligaments and preventing disc compression. 'The macho image of shearers was initially hard to break but they snapped them up once their backs stopped aching,' says Warren, who operates Warrie Shearing Products in Mt Barker, Western Australia. 'Doctors, physiotherapists and chiropractors recommend it; I'm only disappointed the union hasn't made it compulsory. It extends a shearer's working life: those who have been out of the game are going back to it and those that were thinking of giving up are staying in the game.'

This robot, known as Oracle (right), developed by staff of the University of Western Australia's School of Mechanical Engineering, was the first robot to shear a sheep, in 1979. Since then the design has been vastly improved and between 1985 and 1993 the school demonstrated the efficiency of a superior robot — Shear Magic — which is capable of fully automated shearing. The work, developed over fifteen years, was funded entirely by the then Australian Wool Corporation to the tune of $10 million and established an international reputation for Australian robotics research but hit a snag when the wool industry crisis struck. Now there is neither the money nor the confidence to develop commercial applications, which would conservatively cost $100 million. 'The wool industry has not capitalised on what we made available to it,' says Professor James Trevelyan. 'But it was strategic research and the threat of the robot being introduced has kept the cost of shearing down. The wool industry has saved far more than the cost of the robotic research.'

6

PRESENT HISTORICALS

The character of today's wool industry is so firmly rooted in its humble origins that it's difficult to say where the past ends and the present begins. Pride in this strong heritage seeps into every facet of woolgrowing and manufacturing.

The Macarthur homestead at Camden Park (above, right), south-west of Sydney, is now privately owned by descendants of John and Elizabeth Macarthur but visitors can gain an appreciation of the contributions the pair made to the Australian wool industry at adjoining Belgenny Farm. The Macarthurs took up a 5000-acre (2025 hectare) land grant at Camden Park (then called Cowpastures) in 1805 and during John's long absences abroad Elizabeth assumed the role of studmaster. Theirs was Australia's first merino flock to be run on stud principles and many of the practices they developed at Camden Park were eventually adopted throughout the colony.

Geelong's location, close to the rich farming land of the western district, made it a significant port in the 1840s and 1850s and the exports handled by its wharves at one time far exceeded those of Melbourne. Many of the historic buildings that remain of that bustling era are now classified by the National Trust, including the red-brick former wool store (at left) and the 1872 bluestone store (at right), that now houses the National Wool Museum in Moorabool Street. Baled wool delivered to the wool stores first by dray and then by truck was inspected and either purchased directly or by auction. Wool to be shipped to other Australian ports or overseas was railed to the nearby docks for loading. The saw-tooth roof, a bale chute and sections of the original wooden floor are now prized architectural features of the museum building.

'It looks just like it did the day the men stepped out of it; you can still smell the sweat,' says Bob McFarland of the river red gum slab building that now houses the Oxley station museum (opposite). 'I'm also keen to remember all the people who have worked for my family, who have bent their backs and sweated blood, so we're trying to document their contributions, too.' The station's first private home, built in 1834, was later used as men's quarters. It now contains a wonderful collection of station memorabilia and machinery garnered over a century.

Woolmers (opposite) is one of the earliest and largest farming estates in Tasmania, near Longford in the north-east, and a stunning example of the grand mansions financed by wool cheques. The property was established in 1816 by Thomas Archer, who was granted 800 acres (324 hectares) on the banks of the Macquarie River by Governor Macquarie himself. By the 1820s Thomas Archer employed over 50 workers, many of them convicts, and most of the original buildings, furniture and furnishings, and an extensive collection of family memorabilia, firearms, sporting equipment, vehicles, art, farming equipment and photographs survive. The grand dining room (above), once the focal point of entertaining, is furnished almost entirely with Cuban mahogany and features Italianate arches and Thomas Archer's portrait above the black marble mantelpiece. An 80-piece Worcester china service, thought to have been made in 1868, is complemented by 1780s silverware.

Waterworks pioneered by woolgrowers on the creeks and rivers of the Riverina were a contributing inspiration to the development of irrigation schemes in the region. Irrigation pioneer William Benjamin Chaffey lived in the elegant home Rio Vista (right) in Mildura until his death in 1926. Now a museum with original furnishings and fittings, it was first occupied in 1892, shortly after William and his brother George established the Mildura Irrigation Colony upon which many of today's irrigation systems were founded.

All among the wool boys all among the wool
Keep your blades full boys keep your blades full
I can do a respectable tally myself whenever I like to try
And they know me round the blackblocks as Flash Jack from Gundagai.

Local legend has it that the Flash Jack referred to in this anonymous ditty was a man by the name of Jack Davis, but the song's inspiration remains unsubstantiated. What we do know is that woolgrowing has been a lifeblood of the Gundagai economy since its settlement in the late 1830s. Like Hay, the town (opposite) grew up as a major stock crossing point on the Murrumbidgee as vast numbers of would-be pastoralists snatched up runs as they charted the river south-westwards. Large vats at the Gundagai Museum speak of tougher times when sheep were worth nothing more than the price of tallow.

Transport old and new. The stout wool wagon (above) that greets visitors to Kojunup, south of Perth, pays tribute to the pioneers who forged the region's wool industry. Transporting wool to market, mostly by semitrailer, remains one of the costliest components of wool-growing. Many Australian sheep properties are kilometres from the wool stores, auction rooms and docks through which their wool must be handled.

Tired timbers are being restored to their former glory within the Blackall wool scour, in the gidgee scrub of central western Queensland. The steam-powered wool-washing plant (opposite) operated for seventy years from 1908, fed by artesian springs nearby and serviced by a rail line that dispatched the clean wool to Rockhampton or Brisbane. It was one of 52 steam-powered wool scours built in Australia, but the last of those that also had a shearing shed attached. At its busiest the scour ran 24 hours a day and employed about 50 men. Every year from 1913 to 1923 an average of 5267 bales of wool were scoured and more than 135,000 sheep shorn. With the decline in wool scouring in the 1950s shearing kept the Blackall plant alive. Locals hope the restored scour will become a major tourist attraction.

'I saw a lot of the old gear disappearing and thought I'd better save it from the scrap-heap,' says Ron Denney, perched atop his restored Moline universal tractor, circa 1910. He has amassed an impressive collection of engines, shearing plants, handpieces and general farming equipment on his property near Cranbrook, Western Australia, and the private museum can be visited by appointment. Ron counts a single-stand, hand-operated shearing plant among his prized possessions. 'Worksafe would have a coronary over some of these items; we've come a long way in design and technology over the past fifty years.'

The entrance to the Waltzing Matilda Centre (left), at Winton naturally features a statue of the man who penned Australia's unofficial national song. Banjo Paterson reportedly wrote the words while visiting Dagworth station, 80 kilometres north-west of Winton, in January 1895 and it was first sung in public four months later, to the tune of an old Scottish ballad, at the North Gregory Hotel in Winton. Centre manager Ian Jempson says Paterson was clearly influenced by the politics of the day, including the Great Shearers' Strike of 1891, and the song embodies strong elements of the Australian character. 'The verse speaks of self-determination, pride, passion, mateship, the freedom of life on the wallaby and the wonderful potential that Australia offered,' he says.

The western Riverina town of Hay (right) began as a Murrumbidgee River crossing for stock being driven south to the Victorian markets during the gold rushes of the 1850s. The township developed as the commercial hub for surrounding pastoral properties. Until the railway line was extended to the town in 1882 Hay was an important port for river steamers transporting the annual wool-clip. The main street is lined with glorious old buildings and features the Witcombe Fountain — an ornate cast-iron monument presented to the people of Hay in 1883 by the then Mayor, John Witcombe.

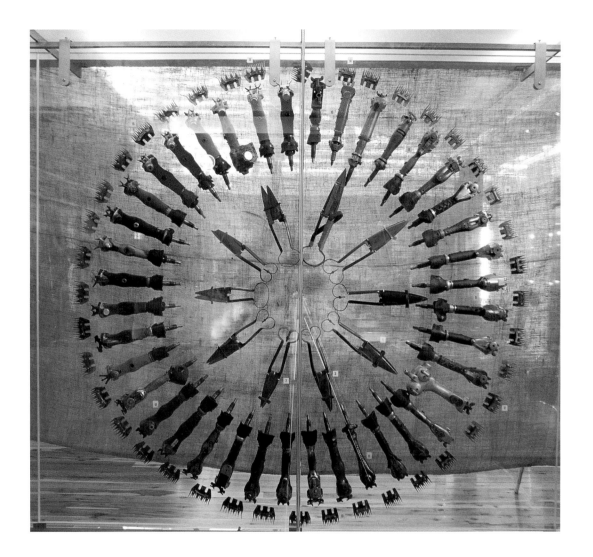

The corrugated iron so typical of shearing sheds across Australia has been employed to great effect (opposite) at Shear Outback, the Australian Shearers' Hall of Fame in Hay. The museum celebrates the contribution that shearers have made to Australia's folklore, culture and economy and features the original Murray Downs shearing shed, which stood on the banks of the Murray River at Swan Hill for more than seventy years. Visitors can also enjoy shearing demonstrations and view a collection of blades and rare Australian and imported mechanical handpieces dating from the 1890s (above) collected from woolsheds in the Southern Tablelands and Riverina by the late Grahame 'Horse' Daniels, of Wagga Wagga.

Teamsters once stopped beside a large waterhole at the stock-route junction that now hosts the Australian Stockman's Hall of Fame and Outback Heritage Centre (following pages). Since opening in 1988 the centre has welcomed some 840,000 visitors with displays dedicated to the pioneers of the Australian outback. A section of a shearing shed, an 1860s settler's hut, a blacksmith's shop and hawker's wagon are among the exhibits, with pure wool carpet, supplied by the then Australian Wool Corporation, underfoot.

Crumbling walls and footings (left) are all that remain of this property near Burra in the heart of South Australian sheep country.

What stories it could tell if only this river red gum (below, left) could talk. Known locally as the Steamer Tree, this 800-year-old veteran was used to lever the Nap Nap station wool bales on to barges for transport down the Murrumbidgee River. Situated on the Lowbidgee floodplain between Hay and Balranald, Nap Nap was settled by George Hobler in about 1845 and originally ranged over 106,110 hectares. Now it's just 36,000 hectares and carries 10,000 sheep and 1500 cattle as well as 4000 hectares of cereal crops. These days the annual clip of about 200 bales travels by semitrailer direct to Melbourne in roughly seven hours.

Stretching out to the horizon, the Fowlers Bay jetty (opposite) played an integral part in the dispatch of wool and other produce to ships that serviced South Australia's west coast. At one time wool was the bay's main export. Until the jetty's construction in 1896 small rowing boats known as 'lighters' ferried wool bales, passengers, supplies and even live sheep out to the larger vessels anchored in the bay. Pastoral leases were first granted in the region in the 1860s and 1870s but were gradually consolidated into the vast Fowlers Bay sheep run that extended from the Nullarbor to Point Brown, near Streaky Bay. After the 1880s, as the pastoral leases were progressively resumed for closer settlement, the area was opened to cereal growing. The jetty, thrice extended, survives as a prime fishing spot.

The influence of sheep on Australia's social and economic life is well remembered in our art and literature. Sheep have been written about, painted, immortalised in song and mythologised by the likes of Henry Lawson, Banjo Paterson and Tom Roberts. Until *Advance Australia Fair* was installed as our national anthem in the 1970s *Waltzing Matilda* and *Click Go the Shears* were widely regarded as our national songs and structures like the Big Merino at Goulburn and the Big Wool Bales at Hamilton in Victoria make an even larger statement. Elsewhere, the passion for sheep and wool is expressed more subtly.

> If I had been a poet, instead of a worker with the brush, I should have described the scattered flocks on sunlit plains and gum-covered ranges, the coming of spring, the gradual massing of the sheep towards the one centre, the woolshed, through which the accumulated growth and wealth of the year is carried; the shouts of the men, the galloping of horses and the barking of dogs as the thousands are driven, half seen, through the hot dust cloud, to the yards; then the final act, and the dispersion of the denuded sheep.

Tom Roberts, circa 1890, referring to his painting, *Shearing the Rams*.

Sculpting offers artist Stephen King welcome relief from the drudgery of sheep-farming, so he relished the challenge to create these regal busts in stringy-bark (left) for the entrance to the Petali Merino Stud, just north of Walcha. 'Carving for me is like a holiday from the farm,' he says. Although several of his larger figurative pieces beautify the Walcha town centre, he'd never before carved a sheep and set out to produce 'proud figureheads'. 'Even now, two years on, they're a car-stopper and we often see people taking photographs,' says Cheryl Oppenheimer who commissioned the work to celebrate her husband Martin's fortieth birthday, and twenty years of breeding merinos at Petali, one of Australia's foremost fine merino studs.

The region's reliance on wool production is recognised by the metal sculpture (right) at the northern entrance to Williams, south-east of Perth.

Hamilton's strong links with the Australian wool industry are reflected in the Big Wool Bales in Coleraine Road and sculptures in the Commonwealth Bank forecourt (pictured) in Gray Street by Tony Trembath. A time capsule placed in the ram tower is due to be opened in 2062, on the two hundreth anniversary of the establishment of the state Bank branch in Hamilton. The Hamilton Art Gallery also has in its collection three woollen tapestries, including the Kossatz Hamilton Wool Tapestry designed by Les Kossatz and woven by the Victorian Tapestry Workshop to mark Victoria's one hundred and fiftieth anniversary.

7

RECREATION

And they're racing!

The people around 'The Junction' still talk of the year when welcome rains washed out the annual race meeting. Swollen creeks kept the thoroughbreds and their jockeys from the track east of Carnarvon, in Western Australia, and the 1000-strong crowd was stuck fast for a week. They had plenty of time to organise a few contests of their own. The Phantom Cup and a scrappy, squabbling swarm of dogs provided some of the most memorable racing on record.

Racegoers dine on stories from the September Gascoyne Junction Races long after the tent city has been dismantled and the last of the mongrel dogs have slinked back home. It's been the same for pretty much every year since the 1920s, with the exception of a devastating drought in 1935–36 and the intervention of war. In a pastoral community where social events are few and far between, the bush race meeting has long offered welcome relief from the stark realities of life on the land. That's why the Junction Race Club committee spend the year flogging raffle tickets, hosting functions and even mustering wild goats to raise money to keep them going. The stakes are high.

Clustered around a red dirt track on Jimba Jimba station, in the lee of the Kennedy Ranges, the people of the district (and a growing number of ring-ins) revel in the opportunity to place a modest bet, share a beer and catch up on a year's worth of gossip. They steal shade from the blistering heat in a motley collection of corrugated iron lean-tos evocatively named The Hilton and Room with a View, and prop up the bar in the popular member's stand. 'Everyone becomes a member on race day,' says Junction Race Club secretary Jane McTaggart.

As the afternoon shadows lengthen they hold their breath during race number 4 — the $7000 Junction Cup — count their meagre winnings and the cost of all those tinnies. At night they dine out of camp ovens, serenade each other by firelight and sleep like logs in rough huts, under canvas or under the stars. Bleary-eyed, they wake on Sunday to a day-long family gymkhana — more horses, more dogs and more laughs. Like similar social events that crackle and fizz throughout the Australian bush, the Gascoyne Junction Races are part of 'the glue that binds the community together.'

It's hot and thirsty work both on and off the grounds (left) at the Murchison Polocrosse Carnival. Local teams play each fortnight throughout the winter season and attend five other carnivals over the course of the year. 'Polocrosse is the only sport up here, apart from the annual Christmas cricket match,' says club president Sandy McTaggart.

Competition is fierce at the annual Murchison Polocrosse Carnival each July (opposite). For twenty years they've been converging on a dusty arena north-east of Geraldton, in Western Australia, for the two-day event. The sport has a big following in the district and normally about 25 teams from across the state compete. 'Before wool collapsed we'd have 30 teams,' says Murchison Polocrosse Club president Sandy McTaggart. 'But when the staff on stations are reduced the jackeroos and governesses are the first to go and they've been the backbone of our teams.'

Beer banter (above). Talk of sheep and shearing and record clips fills the bar of the Conargo Hotel — a popular watering-hole for Riverina woolgrowers and shearers since it opened its doors in 1853. An eclectic collection of artwork depicting sheep adorns the walls.

Shadows lengthen (opposite, top) as the polocrosse day at Murchison comes to a close.

On many of the big stations the shearing cut-out was traditionally marked with a celebration. There was horse racing, cricket matches or sports days and family members all joined in. The annual race meeting at William Creek, in South Australia, continues to serve something of a similar function today for sheep and cattle station workers (opposite, bottom) within a wide radius.

Sam Drummond (top), from Carnarvon, cracks a tinny and a broad smile at the bar (top).

Olympic fever found barbed expression in the member's stand at Gascoyne Junction racetrack in 2000 (bottom).

In the shadow of the finishing line, Gascoyne Junction (opposite).

A junior tug of war is one of the hotly contested events of the race weekend. In the amusing dog race poodles, kelpies and Dobermans line up for a teeth-baring, tail-biting dash past the post.

It's a magic weekend at the Gascoyne Junction races for adults and children alike.

The collapse of wool prices in early 1990 and a desire to provide employment opportunities for the next generation has inspired a raft of new business ventures at Mardathuna station, north-west of Carnarvon in Western Australia. Dudley Maslen, pictured above on the right, showcasing some local plant life to day-trippers, jokes that he is now 'unemployed' but in truth things haven't been busier. Along with running 6000 sheep and 5000 cattle on their 222,750 hectares the family operate a bed and breakfast, real estate business and a tour company that reveals the hidden delights of the Kennedy Range, one of the oldest landmasses on earth. 'We ran an average of 25,000 sheep for twenty years but when things got bad we had to diversify and that's how we've survived,' says Dudley.

The annual Wagin show — Woolorama (right) — is now in its thirtieth year and in 2002 boasted 425 trade fair exhibitors and 1300 stud animal entries. Wool fashion parades, shearing competitions (including the fiercely contested Heiniger 100 and Trans Tasman Challenge) and the three-day sheepdog trials are among the major drawcards for some 25,000 visitors each March. Ribbons for the best merinos and British breeds are highly coveted.

The Perth Royal Agricultural Show (opposite) sprawls across the royal showgrounds at Claremont each September–October, continuing a tradition that began with the formation of the Royal Agricultural Society of Western Australia in 1831. It is the state's largest annual community event and features 29 competitive sections. For stock breeders, show competition is the culmination of many years hard work.

The Afghan cameleers responsible for carting much of the wool-clip out of the sandy country of South Australia were the first to frequent what we now know as the William Creek Hotel (top). Built in 1887 it was initially a boarding house before it earned a liquor license in 1938. With the gradual changeover from sheep to cattle in the district, most of the pub's visitors these days are tourists. It does a brisk trade during the annual fun day and gymkhana and whenever nearby Lake Eyre fills with water.

Everyone leaves their mark at the Tilpa Hotel (below), on the banks of the Darling River, north-east of Wilcannia — but it will cost you a $2 donation to the Royal Flying Doctor Service.

The first hotel license was taken up in 1898 and the pub has been a regular haunt of cockies and shearers ever since, with some teams travelling in from 100 kilometres distant to slake their thirst during the customary post-shearing shout. With a population of just 10 the town relies on the hotel for much of its fun. The Tilpa Quickshear, held each July, is big on the social calendar and sees some of Australia and New Zealand's best shearers compete for a $6000 prize pool.

The rewards are lucrative for the first past the post in the Carnarvon Cup, held each September at the Massey Bay Racetrack (opposite). It's the highlight of the racing calendar in the region, where competition among horse breeders for the $16,000 purse is just as intense as that demonstrated by the snappily dressed spectators entering the Fashions in the Field. Superior style wins a Balinese holiday.

Water of any description, be it a billabong, river, creek, waterhole or dam, provides a welcome relief and a place of refuge from the dry dusty conditions experienced on many sheep farming properties.

A saddlebronc rider defies gravity at a rodeo in the Kimberley, Western Australia.

8

SALES & EXPORT

To maintain its place as the world's leading wool producer for 130 years the Australian industry has had to be progressive, from the genetics of sheep breeding through to the technology employed for wool handling, testing and processing. Advances in pasture improvement, artificial insemination, fibre research, transport methods and wool processing have kept pace with the international demand for our wool.

Although Australian flock numbers are down on previous years, our country continues to produce about 70 per cent of the world's finest wool and exports earned our economy over $4 billion in 2001–02.

Bidding gets underway at the Adelaide Plains Livestock Exchange (above), the biggest market for meat sheep in South Australia. Weekly sales see some 25,000 sheep and lambs from most parts of the state and western New South Wales go through the yards. Up to 70 per cent of them are trade and store lambs. Last financial year the exchange handled more than 1.1 million sheep and lambs and 100,000 pigs; the annual turnover from sheep alone was more than $755.8 million.

It's a full house at the Katanning saleyard (opposite), in south-western Western Australia, where some 20,000 head of sheep are sold each Wednesday. It's the biggest regional sale in the state, rivalled only by the Midlands sale on the outskirts of Perth, and in 2001 the Katanning yards processed 1,002,365 sheep, mainly for sale to abattoirs and live export companies. Wesfarmers Landmark agents have the lion's share of business.

The variation in fleece colour is discernible from pen to pen at the Adelaide Plains Livestock Exchange, where sheep from the high rainfall Adelaide Hills mix it with cousins from the drier pastoral zones. The palette of hues is due to differences in soil type, climate, dust penetration and vegetable matter. 'Some are raised on green grass and others on parched paddocks,' says saleyard manager Michael Blight.

A tin dog, a mechanical device which emits a tinny sound, is used to drive sheep through the pens at the Adelaide Plains Livestock Exchange. Trucks start arriving each Monday for the Tuesday sales and there's a steady procession of stock until their departure on Wednesday. Four agents operate at the yards and most of the sheep are sold to abattoirs within South Australia and across the border in Horsham, and to smaller butchers and growers. 'Lamb prices have been quite good for some time and business has been brisk,' says saleyard manager Michael Blight. 'It's been a seller's market and competition in the auction system has seen some good returns for producers.'

A high-class beauty salon for rams or Mahony's Motel, whatever you call it the Mahony Ram Shed caters well to its prestigious clients. What started as a retirement hobby for Roy Mahony (pictured) has become a full-time job for him and his wife Coral at Narrogin, in Western Australia. They specialise in preparing rams for local and interstate shows, sales and field days. During their 11-month stay in a purpose-built shed each ram is pampered; they are fed special diets and weighed each month, have their feet trimmed, their fleece blade-clipped and enjoy daily outings in grassed enclosures for a dose of sunshine. With 20 stud clients throughout the state, the ram shed is almost always at full occupancy — 53 rams — and they are ever-ready to be viewed by potential buyers. 'It's a labour of love,' says Roy. 'You get attached to them throughout the year and when you see the owners pick up big awards you feel a little pride.'

Bidding is brisk for the Wesfarmers Landmark sales team at the Katanning ram sale, one of the most prestigious in Australia. Major studs usually put up about 150 of their elite rams each August and it's not uncommon for the top sires to attract telephone bids from interstate and overseas. A top price of $65,000 was paid for a ram in recent years. Sheep breeders buy in reputable rams to introduce a new feature (such as higher fleece weight) to their flock, to bring about an overall improvement or to enable them to better meet market demands.

Junior judging events like this at Woolorama (right) — Western Australia's largest and most glamorous merino show held annually at Wagin — are designed to develop industry leaders of the future. Many entrants are agricultural students and the merinos and fleece classes are growing in popularity. 'It gives them a solid grounding, to get the feel and look of wool,' says steward Gary Hamersley. 'Some of the more successful entrants have gone on to judge merinos in the eastern states and to become stud breeders themselves.'

Prize ribbons beckon as judging commences at a Riverina sheep show (below, right). Such sheep shows remain a good opportunity for studs to promote their stock but on-property sales and field days are increasingly favoured, partly due to concerns about disease. Studmasters also prefer to conduct sales in their own environment, where they have a captive audience and can also display ewes, lambs and fleeces, and give potential clients a tour of their property.

Dozens of trucks prepare to unload sheep at the Fremantle docks (opposite) for live export to Kuwait. This multideck container ship can carry 80,000 head and is one of about 10 that travel constantly between Western Australia and the Middle East with loads that vary from 35,000 to 135,000 sheep. Live export from Australia (so that sheep can be slaughtered overseas according to religious custom) began with the shipment of 16,000 sheep in 1962 and today earns Australia nearly $250 million a year. Over six million sheep and lambs are exported live to the Middle East annually, of which about 70 per cent are exported from Western Australia, 16 per cent from Victoria and 12 per cent from South Australia. 'Prices have doubled in the last 18 months but there continues to be a strong demand,' says David Kerr, livestock manager for Wellard Rural, a major live sheep exporting company. 'We have buyers roaming the country and we bring the sheep into feedlots, where they are acclimatised for seven days before departure.'

Serious deliberations as judges (from left to right) George McKenzie, David Webster, Ray Wise, John Crawford and Peter Frost confer during the 2002 Sydney Sheep Show held at Sydney's Royal Easter Show. The tradition of showing livestock in Australia dates back to 1823, when the Agricultural Society of New South Wales conducted the first 'agricultural exhibition' at Parramatta in October. Hannibal Macarthur (nephew of John and Elizabeth) purportedly won the first prize ever for sheep in Australia with five merino rams. Agricultural societies proliferated with the interest in improved sheep breeding from the 1870s onwards and the Parramatta exhibition developed into what we now know as the Sydney Royal Easter Show. Sheep are judged according to their conformation, the evenness of fleece coverage, trueness to type and wool quality. 'We're looking for stud sheep that will have an impact on the industry,' says sheep judge of twenty years experience John Crawford.

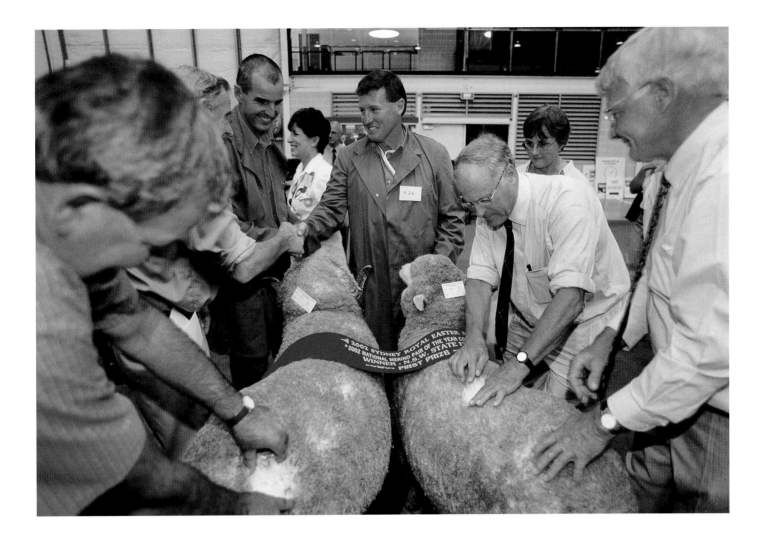

A winning smile from Russell Jones, owner of Darriwell Merino Stud at Trundle, New South Wales, as he accepts congratulations for his New South Wales state finalists in the National Merino Pair of the Year during the 2002 Sydney Sheep Show. In the early days of sheep breeding, shows were enormously influential, providing a chance to compare stock, exchange ideas on animal husbandry and share innovative practices. They were a benchmark for measuring excellence in breeding and the reputations of the big-name studs were won or lost on the number of show ribbons they collected. Showing remains equally important today for professional and social reasons, recognising sometimes a lifetime's devotion to sheep breeding.

Peter Ritter (above) of Dunumbral station near Collarenabri gets down to business with stock and wool specialist Carl Carlon in the drafting yards. In the age of emails, faxes and telephones, such face-to-face contact remains an important part of the wool industry. It represents an opportunity for the grower to discuss sale options, negotiate actual sales and learn about industry advances. 'We get stuck in our own little world sometimes,' says Dunumbral manager Cameron Ritter. 'We value whatever we can find out from the agents; they're buying and selling wool all the time.' Most of Dunumbral's clip is sold at auction in Newcastle but the Ritters have the option of selling direct to wool specialists like Carl.

'What's all this about, then?' Rams watch a sale in progress (opposite) on a private property near Mount Barker in Western Australia. Sheep pass on many of their characteristics to their progeny in a very pure way so the ram has most influence on the flock because he is capable of producing far more lambs than a single ewe. The selection of rams for breeding is therefore vitally important, both within a stud and in a commercial flock, and they are chosen not only for their superiority in the current generation but for their ability to pass on those characteristics to their offspring. Early breeding programs concentrated on desirable characteristics in individual rams. Now artificial insemination and in-vitro fertilisation can give much greater control and wider distribution of productive genes.

Woolgrower and agent Tom Redden (left) loads wool bound for Port Adelaide with help from (left to right) Chris Callery, Levi Pligi, and his son Matthew Redden. Tom runs about 7000 medium-wool merinos and crossbreds on his property near Hamley Bridge in South Australia to produce 120 bales a year. Wool is warehoused and tested in Adelaide but Tom can no longer sell his clip there. Instead, samples are sent to Melbourne or Sydney and sold at auction there. Once the sale has been finalised the bales are dispatched direct from the Adelaide port.

Tri-packs — three bales of greasy wool compressed together — were developed in Australia to save money on shipping costs. Freight charges are calculated per shipping container so the more compact the bales, the bigger the load that each container can carry.

The erection and maintenance of fences is one of the major costs of any sheep-farming operation. The more popular prefabricated fencing like this (above) costs about $1800 to $2000 per kilometre, compared to $1000 to $1200 per kilometre for the plain wire and barb style, which isn't nearly as effective at containing sheep. Other major on-farm costs include fuel, fertiliser, animal health (drench, husbandry, etc), shearing and, in higher rainfall areas, pasture improvements.

Sunbeam Australia, now owned by Tru-Test, has celebrated one hundred years in the wool industry and remains the largest supplier of shearing equipment to the world. It is Larry Eldridge's task to spray-paint the handles of every handpiece (opposite), many of which are exported to the likes of Europe, England, South Africa and New Zealand. The company also manufactures overhead gear, combs, cutters and grinders.

Fleece testing contractor Ashley Lock oversees the classing of poll merino rams (top) with Tony Hamersley, owner of the Haseley Poll Merino Stud, one hundred kilometres north-east of Perth. Ashley travels with a mobile OFDA 2000 unit that is capable of delivering fleece measurements in seconds in the race or on the shearing board. 'Up until about three years ago I had to take a fleece sample and send it to the Australian Wool Testing Authority and it would take up to a fortnight to get the reading,' says Tony. 'Having fibre diameter measurements done on the day enables us to cull and class at the same time, saving considerable time mustering. It has been quite a revolution, particularly with the drive to breed finer woolled sheep; it's a fine-tuning of the traditional visual assessment.'

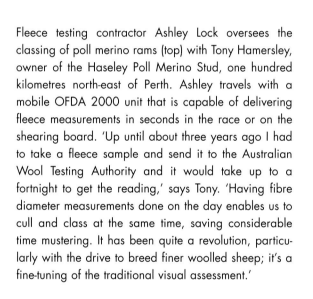

The telephone, fax and internet services may have revolutionised some aspects of business, but woolgrowers still value personal service. Here Wesfarmers Landmark area wool manager and Northern New South Wales merino stud stock manager John Croake (bottom) discusses the merits of the company's genetics library with Lachlan Fulloon, studmaster of Cressbrook Merino Stud. John clocks up about 100,000 kilometres a year liaising with clients. 'They're not just clients; they're friends as well and on-farm service is critically important,' says John. 'About half my clients are on-line, doing their banking, watching their shares and emailing colleagues but they still like face-to-face contact.'

Fine-wool growing remains an economic mainstay of Yass, as demonstrated by this store in the main street. Settlement dates back to the mid-1820s, when explorers Hamilton Hume and William Hovell issued favourable reports of the fertile plains they passed through as they sought an overland route to Port Phillip Bay.

Laurie Walsh supervises the sampling of wool bales at a Newcastle wool store for testing by the Australian Wool Testing Authority Ltd (AWTA). The AWTA was established in 1957 to provide objective information to woolgrowers, processors and buyers on the key price-determining characteristics of wool — a major change for an industry steeped in tradition and subjectivity. Its role expanded rapidly with the introduction of new test methods and the Sale by Sample selling system in the 1970s. This allowed woolgrowers to present their wool for sale on the basis of objective test information, rather than traditional visual appraisal. In the sales arena, regardless of how it is marketed, virtually all Australian wool to be sold is certified by the AWTA for yield, fibre diameter, staple length and staple strength, and sold on the basis of that certification. The AWTA also tests wool subsequent to sale for exporters, wool scourers and carbonisers, processors, the textile trade and research organisations. 'With the benefit of AWTA certification growers are assured of being paid according to the objective specification of their wool and wool processors can confidently expect that wool purchased to their price and processing specifications will perform to their requirements,' says AWTA managing director Michael Jackson.

A technician with the Australian Wool Testing Authority Ltd tests for wool grease. Wool sampling is conducted by the AWTA in 38 cities and towns throughout Australia and samples are sent to one of its three raw wool testing laboratories — in Melbourne, Sydney and Perth. The labs process hundreds of thousands of tests each year and all AWTA certified results are issued in accordance with international standards. This presale test information is transmitted electronically to wool brokers for inclusion in sale catalogues, allowing growers to consider their options prior to sale. The information also provides the grower with objective feedback on on-farm management practices.

About 30 auctions a year are held within the timbered walls of the Fremantle Wool Exchange (top) — the only auction house of its kind in Western Australia. As at most Australian wool auctions the majority of buyers represent or are employed by the major overseas processing companies (largely based in China, India, Italy and western Europe) and except for a small proportion processed by Jandakot Wool Washing and a similar quantity trucked across the Nullarbor for processing in the eastern states, all the wool sold in Fremantle — about 28 per cent of the national clip — is destined to be exported greasy.

The first wool auction in Australia was held in 1840 in Adelaide, followed by sales in Sydney in 1843, Melbourne in 1848, Brisbane in 1898, Hobart in 1902 and Perth in 1913. While the auction system managed by the Australian Wool Exchange remains the most common means of selling wool some growers are now negotiating direct sales to processors.

The traditional way of valuing wool prior to 1972 was a time-consuming and labour intensive business. Entire wool bales spewed forth their fluffy contents on showroom floors across the country and potential buyers relied on their own visual assessments of the fleeces under natural light streaming in through saw-tooth roofs. This was superseded by today's Sale by Sample method, whereby samples for each sale lot are displayed in boxes (bottom) and AWTA fleece yield (the percentage of total weight that is wool), fibre diameter, and staple length and strength measurements are presented in a sale catalogue. Buyers like this one at the Wesfarmers Landmark section of the wool show floor near Melbourne examine the test information in the catalogue, appraise the samples of lots that interest them (known as 'fondling the fibre') and then bid at auction for these lots. About 80 per cent of Australia's wool is sold at auction this way; the remainder is sold privately, through forward contracting or via the electronic system. The Melbourne store is one of the nation's busiest, drawing bales from South Australia, the southern Riverina, Tasmania and Victoria. Nationwide, the shift from spring to autumn shearing or sometimes two shearings a year has largely removed peaks in the receival patterns at wool stores.

WOOL MANUFACTURING

The bulk of Australia's raw wool continues to be exported to overseas processors. While a number of large Australian companies do first-stage processing of greasy wool into tops (cleaned and combed wool), only a handful spin and weave woollen yarn into finished fabric.

Greasy wool is processed in one of two main ways — the worsted system or the woollen system. The majority of Australian wool is processed using the worsted system to produce smooth woven or fine knit fabrics for high-quality clothing. The best part of the fleece is called combing wool and it is scoured, carded, combed into thick strands called slivers, drawn, spun, knitted, woven, dyed and finished.

The woollen system uses the shorter wool fibres that may have been contaminated with burrs or seeds to produce hairier yarn for socks, blankets, upholstery and bulky knitwear. This process involves scouring, carbonising, carding, spinning, knitting, weaving, dyeing and finishing.

Wash and wear. A sheep dip of a different kind (above, left) at Jandakot Wool Washing in Western Australia. About 65 per cent of Australia's wool is exported as greasy wool (above, right) but the remaining 35 per cent of raw wool (about 192 million kilograms in 2001–2002) is scoured and/or made into tops before further processing in Australia or being exported to overseas processors.

Jandakot (opposite) is one of 12 scours operating across Australia and the only one in Western Australia. It has the capacity to produce some 25 million tonnes of clean wool each year for its clients, many of whom are wool buyers with contracts to sell clean wool overseas. Scouring removes natural grease, sweat, dirt and other contaminants. The amount of foreign matter wool contains varies according to the type and breed of sheep, the pasture on which they have been grazed, the soil type and climatic conditions. Raw wool usually contains up to 35 per cent by weight of lanolin (natural grease) and impurities. There have been some technological advances but the actual process of washing wool remains little changed from that practised a century ago. Two of the greatest advancements have been improvements to the efficiency of water usage and the management of effluent. At the Jandakot scour three washing lines operate; an older model pictured in the foreground, with a more modern line at left. During scouring the wool is washed thoroughly in hot water and biodegradable detergent, rinsed and then dried.

Topsoil and plant residue recovered from Australia's premier wool-growing districts during scouring at the Geelong Wool Combing plant is now finding its way back to nature. Since 1998 GWC has been converting its production waste into a high-grade organic soil conditioner and organic fertiliser — over 25,000 cubic metres a year — and marketing it to nurseries, market gardeners and orchardists. Growing trials have shown that topsoil delivers significant amounts of nitrogen and potassium, improves soil moisture retention, reduces soil erosion and promotes soil aeration, which enables better root penetration and growth. Before this recycling initiative the by-product of wool washing was disposed as landfill.

Freshly combed wool leaves one of the 52 combing machines at Geelong Wool Combing. Having been scoured, carded to remove vegetable matter and made into slivers, the slivers are drafted to align the fibres in preparation for combing. The combing process then removes all the short fibres and any remaining impurities to produce wool tops. GWC is in the business of converting greasy wool into high-quality tops for use by overseas spinners of worsted or knitted yarns. It processes over 100,000 wool bales each year to produce about 10 million kilograms of wool tops, most of which is destined for markets in Asia and Europe.

The modern combing mill of Michell Australia — the largest processor and exporter of Australian wool — is a model of efficiency. Based in the Adelaide suburb of Salisbury, Michell buys about 20 per cent of Australia's annual wool-clip (almost half a million bales) and employs more than 900 people in the processing of up to 750 tonnes of wool a week. The vast majority of its wool tops, carbonised and scoured wools and greasy wools are exported to clients in 50 countries, and the company turns over more than $500 million annually. 'Our aim is to ensure that spinners, weavers and knitters receive the quality top they require to achieve optimum performance,' says Michell Australia chairman John Michell. It's a far cry from the modest operation started at Undalya in 1870 by George Henry Michell. He persuaded local growers to sell their wool direct to him, then washed, dried and packed the wool by hand and delivered it to Adelaide for shipment to the London auctions.

An Axminster carpet loom built in England by Brintons in 1910 is the centrepiece of the National Wool Museum in Geelong, which celebrates Australia's wool heritage through a series of interactive displays. This gripper loom uses a jacquard system for weaving colours, whereby punched cards instruct the loom on the colours to use. It was used for fifteen years in Brintons' Geelong factory until it was replaced in 1975. The museum also features three permanent galleries relating to woolgrowing, processing and wool innovations. Visitors can buy carpets made on the loom or socks courtesy of the museum's sock-knitting machine.

The first step in turning cleaned and combed wool, known as tops, into fabric is to produce spinning yarn. At Macquarie Textiles at Albury, Australia's largest woollen and worsted manufacturing facility, compressed tops are drawn into thin threads and twisted together in spinning machines like the one pictured above. Wool threads may be blended with other fibres and dyed at this stage. The yarn is then wound onto large bobbins ready for knitting and/or weaving (right).

A warping machine (above) transfers spun yarn through a weave shed before it is woven into fabric at Macquarie Textiles. The mill processes around 2.5 million kilograms of clean woollen fibre annually, converting it into some 5 million metres of woven fabric and some 500 tonnes of knitting yarn. Its main products are apparel, furnishings and blankets for the domestic market, as well as export to Japan, the United States, Hong Kong, Canada, Taiwan, England, Germany, China and many other Asian-Pacific countries.

A Macquarie Textiles worker (left) inspects fabric for flaws and mends them on the spot. This is one of the final stages in a production process that involves blending, carding, combing and drawing woollen fibres before they are spun and woven, the yarn dyed, and fabric produced and finished.

Tapestry artist-weavers (above), seated from left to right, Grazyna Bleja, Milena Paplinska and Georgina Barker discuss their work with a visitor to the Victorian Tapestry Works. Australia's only tapestry studio, established in 1976, employs weavers full-time to make large-scale tapestries for private homes, institutions and corporate and government buildings. The material of choice is Australian wool, specifically Corriedale-cross fleeces, which are selected for their long, straight fibres, even diameter, and resistance to fluffing and pilling. All the tops wool used in the studio is sourced from Macquarie Textiles in Albury. The colourful piece they are working on was modelled on John Olsen's *Sun Rising Over Australia Felix*, while the Christopher Pyett work *Late Evening By the Water* was the inspiration for this work (opposite). Once completed, the tapestries are treated only for mothproofing and live long, illustrious lives.

A selection of hand-made woollen garments are just one of the attractions of the Wool Centre at Ross, in central Tasmania. As well as the retail outlet, the centre features a wool exhibition area (including a large mural of a 1920s shearing shed and a 'touch and feel' display) and a museum that documents the wool industry from settlement to today.

It's truly fashion on the farm at Wentworth station, near Young, where sheep farmer–fashion designer Vince Nowlan conjures up curvaceous designs from his home-grown wool. Pictured in the historic shearing shed are (left to right) Sophie Nowlan, Laura and Kristy Walton (modelling a top designed by Vince), and Amelia Nowlan. Vince, a father of five, discovered his design flair in 1997, in the face of plummeting wool prices. 'Things were pretty tight so I looked at ways of making extra money,' he says. Vince's wife Tracey now manufactures his designs marketed under the Wentworth Organic Wool label and the garments are sold through stockists in Sydney and Canberra. 'We're keen to keep it in the family but we are looking at markets in New York,' says Vince, who has a number of design awards to his credit and was invited in 2001 to show at the Australian Mercedes Fashion Awards. 'That's not bad for a sheep farmer.'

Woollen garments find favour on the catwalk (above) at the Sydney Royal Easter Show. For seven years the show has hosted the finalists of the Australian Wool Fashion Awards — a major promotion for Australian wool and an opportunity for designers and dressmakers to have their work judged by some of Australia's leading designers. More than 70 per cent of the world's wool ends up as fashion clothing — because it is readily dyed, keeps its shape, drapes beautifully and can be manufactured in a wide variety of weights and weaves. Wool is also prized because it is resilient and flame resistant, a good insulator, absorbent, blends well with other fibres and is relatively free of static electricity.

The upmarket Italy-based apparel manufacturer Ermenegildo Zegna has been a major buyer of Australia's superfine merino wools since its foundation in 1910. For the past thirty-nine years Zegna has sponsored keenly contested national awards aimed at encouraging Australian producers to continue to strive for lower micron wool. Zegna's fabrics and garments, like this stylish men's suit (opposite), are renowned worldwide for their quality and creativity. In addition to Australian merino wool, Zegna uses Inner Mongolian cashmere and South African kid mohair.

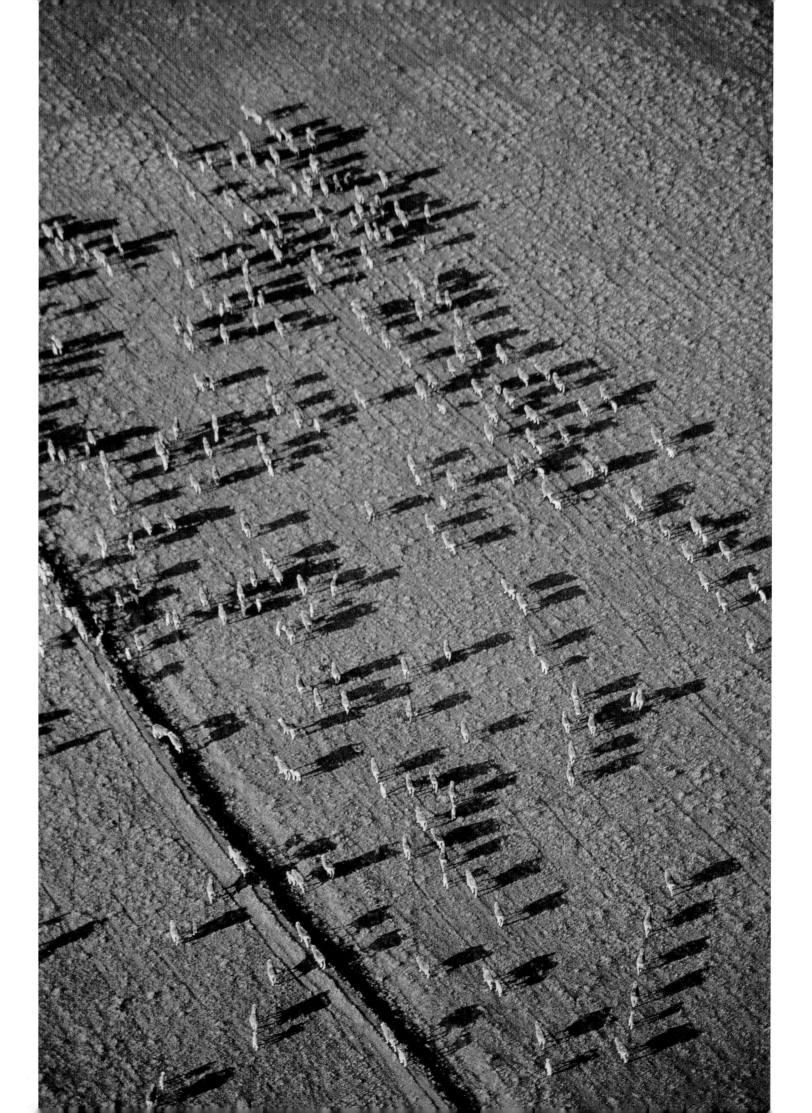

PHOTOGRAPHIC ACKNOWLEDGEMENTS

Acknowledgement is due for the use of some of the photographs used in this book:
Pages 9, 10, 13 (top) are with the courtesy of The State Library of South Australia; pages 18, 20 (below), 26 (top) are with the courtesy of The State Library of New South Wales; pages 11, 12, 13 (below), 14, 16 (top), 16 (below), 20 (top), 26 (below), 32 (below) are with the courtesy of The National Library of Australia; page 31 with permission from the Waltzing Matilda Museum, Winton, Queensland; page 15 by Judy White; page 97 (top) by Jeff Carter; pages 202, 203, 225 by Phil Quirk, Wildlight; page 217 with permission from Geelong Wool Combing Ltd; page 218 with permission from Michell Australia; page 226 by Andrew Stephenson, Wildlight; and page 227 with permission from Ermenegildo Zegna.

INDEX